THE JOY OF WRITING SEX

ELIZABETH BENEDICT

STORY PRESS
CINCINNATI, OHIO

The Joy of Writing Sex: A Guide for Fiction Writers. Copyright © 1996 by Elizabeth Benedict. Printed and bound in the United States of America. All rights reserved. No part of this book may be reproduced in any form or by any electronic or mechanical means including information storage and retrieval systems without permission in writing from the publisher, except by a reviewer, who may quote brief passages in a review. Published by Story Press, an imprint of F&W Publications, Inc., 1507 Dana Avenue, Cincinnati, Ohio 45207. (800) 289-0963. First edition.

Other fine Story Press Books are available from your local bookstore or direct from the publisher.

00 99 98 97 96   5 4 3 2 1

Library of Congress Cataloging-in-Publication Data

Benedict, Elizabeth.
    The joy of writing sex : a guide for fiction writers / by Elizabeth Benedict.—
1st ed.
        p.   cm.
    Includes index.
    ISBN 1-884910-21-1
    1. Fiction—Authorship. 2. Fiction—Technique. I. Title.
PN3355.B38   1996
808.3—dc20   96-7333
                                                                      CIP

Designed by Clare Finney
Cover illustration by Celia Johnson

The permissions opposite this page constitute an extension of this copyright page.

PERMISSIONS

This is for Jerome Badanes (1937-1995), who taught me that sometimes it has to be over the top to be in the right place, and for Lee Goerner (1947-1995), who cared about every last word.

ACKNOWLEDGMENTS

We think of sex as something done in very small groups, and sometimes all alone, but writing about writing about sex has more closely resembled an orgy that grew larger by the week. I could not have put together *The Joy of Writing Sex* without the brains, brawn, good humor and e-mail of many friends, colleagues and near strangers, who offered book titles and ideas, who listened patiently to mine, who photocopied stories, and lent, bought and gave me books, in some cases, with yellow stick-on notes jutting out like unruly bookmarks, alerting me to the exact location of the dirty parts.

Everyone I spoke to, but especially the writers who were generous enough to take time to be interviewed and who answered my letters, helped me figure out what to tell you about how to write about sex.

I owe special thanks to editor in chief of Story Press, Lois Rosenthal, who called one afternoon and rescued me from the uncertainties of beginning a new novel with an offer that, as you can see, I could not refuse. In addition to being paid to read sexy books and think for long periods of nothing but sex, another perk of writing this book is that I have always had something to talk about at dinner parties that *everyone* wants to weigh in on, which is more than can be said of writing a novel. I am certain I will never have it so good, conversation-wise, as I did while writing this book.

Jack Heffron has been a patient, diligent and good-humored editor, helping me to focus, organize and get to the instructional point.

I'm indebted to Lisa Meyer, whose early reading of the introduction prodded me on; to Goldberry Long, for her long-distance research; to Pinckney Benedict, who sent his student Alice Lukens to me; to Deborah Eisenberg, who sent her student Ian McGuire to me; to Stephen Wright, for schlepping a copy of *The Good Parts* from Tower Records; to Jean Hanff Korelitz for a close reading of the manuscript; to Joanne Omang for another; to Katherine Meyer, Liz Forster, Kit Ward and Joe Gangemi for great suggestions; to Carol Houck Smith and her assistant at W.W. Norton, who led this horse to water with a bunch of yellow stick-on notes inside some very fine fiction; to Anne Hindley, for help with French from England; and to Michael Wood, who knew the answers to several arcane and essential literary and linguistic questions.

Richard McCann read an early draft of the chapter on writing about sex in the age of AIDS and guided me through the revision with the luminous intelligence and generosity he brings to all our encounters.

The two friends who share the dedication page died unexpectedly within thirty-six hours of each other as I was completing my work. They never met, but they shared an abiding devotion to literature and to the mysterious, magical process of good writing that I hope this book honors and encourages.

My colleagues at Princeton have been generous to the point of indulgence. I am particularly grateful to Ruth Carden for helping ease some of the technical burdens of writing this book.

As always, Gail Hochman and Marianne Merola are agents from heaven.

To my family and to the usual suspects, from A. to Z., my gratitude knows no bounds.

CONTENTS

It is a bawdy planet.
> — Shakespeare
> *The Winter's Tale*

Sex does not thrive on monotony. Without feelings, inventions, moods, [there are] no surprises in bed. Sex must be mixed with tears, laughter, words, promises, scenes, jealousy, envy, all the spices of fear, foreign travel, new faces, novels, stories, dreams, fantasies, music, dancing, opium, wine.
> — Anaïs Nin
>> From a letter, reprinted in her diary, to the man paying her one dollar a page to write erotic stories.

Anyone who attempts to render sexual experience directly must face the fact that the writhings which comprise it are ludicrous without their subjective content.
> — William Gass
> *On Being Blue*

INTRODUCTION

I was given permission to write about sex in my fiction long before I knew how badly I would need it. In my sophomore year at Barnard, three graduates returned one afternoon to tell us about their careers as writers. They spoke in a science lecture hall with the periodic table of the elements hanging behind them and me in the front row, hanging on their every word; even then I knew I wanted to do what they did. One was a perky blonde-haired poet with a Chinese name, class of '63, whose first novel was about to be published. I don't remember much of what she said that day in 1973, but of course I remember her name. Erica Jong.

Several months later *Fear of Flying* erupted into all of our lives. On every page, Jong's saucy heroine Isadora Wing celebrated orgasms, infidelity, masturbation, and something truly revolutionary called "the Zipless Fuck," which happened when you met a man on a train, had sex with him *right there*, and never saw him again—or even wanted to! That women, nice girls with college degrees, thought these things, did these things, and *said* them in print—it is impossible to convey today how mind-boggling a notion this was for those of us raised, not so long ago, to believe we would be virgins when we got married. Jong's broadcast was a little like learning Nancy Reagan had consulted an astrologer about matters of state while she was First Lady. You have blundered through life thinking the world operates *like this*, and someone comes along and tells you that you are not even close.

At nineteen, I didn't know enough about sex or writing to do much with the freedoms that were now mine for the taking, but I knew this was not business as usual. I knew to pay attention to the uproar and upheaval that Jong and the women's movement had ignited. I knew there was something in it for me as a woman and as a writer. Women's rights and women's sexual pleasure were now front-page news, the nitty-gritty details debated passionately and publicly. The female orgasm had become the symbol and substance of who controlled language, women's bodies and, as it turned out, everything else. In books, broadsides, and the pages of a new magazine called *Ms.*, we pondered real orgasms versus fake, clitoral versus vaginal, Freud versus Masters and Johnson, yours versus mine. Freud lost a lot of standing in this debate for having claimed that a clitoral orgasm was "immature" and a vaginal orgasm was "mature," but the reputation of the Greek sage Tiresias was burnished. Having been both man and woman, he was asked by the gods which gender enjoyed sex more. He told them that women got nine times more pleasure than men and was promptly blinded for his trouble. His candor was not much more welcome in Puritan North America, until Isadora Wing admitted to us how she could "come and come and come. . . ."

The sexual tenor of the time, place and family in which we grew up is marked indelibly on our psyches; whether we embrace it or struggle mightily to reject it, when we turn our energies to writing fiction, it travels with us. Before you turn your attention to the body of this book, take some time to reflect on the sexual attitudes of the family and culture in which you were raised. Free associate with pen in hand or sitting at the computer. You might unearth material or gain insight into what makes you and your characters tick when the narrative veers in the direction of the boudoir. Novelist Stephen Harrigan told me that "the abhorrence of sex" drilled into him by his education in Catholic schools in the 1950s makes writing every sex scene "a declaration of independence." Though he was raised to believe he would burn in hell for having impure thoughts, it's his job to have them, he says, "and it's worth risking going to hell to get the scene right."

For those of us who came of age in the early 1970s, in more secular circles, the human body, the sexual connection, was what Henry James would have called our *donnée*, our subject, the idea given us at the outset. Once I started to write seriously, in my early twenties, it never occurred to me *not* to write about sex, any more than it would have occurred to the Romantics not to write about meadows, streams and nightingales. And it never occurred to me that I would not be permitted to say whatever I wanted. But of course, the thaw had been a long, long time coming. It was not until the 1960s that fiction writers could write about sex without the threat of censorship, without the reality of censorship, the prosecutions, trials, jail sentences, bannings, confiscated books, and the incalculable tragedies of self-censorship and silence. It was not until the 1960s that writers could delete the clichés, vagueness, codings and tortured indirection that even the best of them resorted to when they knew that plain speaking might land them behind bars.

None of this is to say that writing about sex is per se a good thing. I don't believe that it is, per se. But it is a bad thing to be prohibited from writing about it and just as bad to *feel* prohibited, whether you fear the long arm of the law, the ghost of your grandmother, the remembered wrath of your minister, or the day-to-day insecurities of the man or woman you live with.

If you have a good working relationship with your censors, internal or external, *The Joy of Writing Sex* aims to help you learn how to show these demons the door. It was also written for those fiction writers who are simply puzzled and uncertain—without being especially inhibited—about what they can possibly say about sex in their fiction at a time when we have the freedom to say whatever we please, but when, as novelist Carol Shields wrote in a letter to me, "the language of sensuality has become so eroded by popular culture." In other words, now that we can say anything, what else is there to say and how do we say it?

The Joy of Writing Sex is not a primer for writing pornography and not a collection of tips for writing hot sex scenes, encounters to excite you and/or your readers on lonely winter nights. The book aims to help you write well about sex—whether the sex is great, obligatory or unwelcome, whether it fizzles, makes you laugh or makes you weep—in fiction that is about something other than the mechanics of sex.

As near as I can define it, the difference between pornography and the kind of sex writing I focus on here is that to the extent you remember anything when pornography is over, you remember the intensity of the orgasms the otherwise unmemorable characters had, or you had. In pornography, consumers will demand their money back if the sex is lousy (i.e., the guy doesn't come) or the girl cries when it's over. This other kind of sex writing thrives on all the things that nourish good fiction: tension, dramatic conflict, character development, insights, metaphors and surprises. You don't have to have read too much of it to know that there is nothing more predictable than pornography.

As with all good fiction writing—and all good sex—there are no rules or formulas for exactly what to do and how to do it, no recipes that guarantee your soufflé will rise every time. What I offer here instead is a comprehensive way of thinking about, writing about and reading sex scenes culled from my twenty years of writing novels and short stories, ten years of teaching writing, and this past year of reading stacks of sex-filled fiction. My four organizing principles are these:

- A good sex scene is not always about good sex, but it is always an example of good writing.
- A good sex scene should always connect to the larger concerns of the work.
- The needs, impulses and histories of your characters should drive a sex scene.
- The relationship your characters have to one another—whether they are adulterers or strangers on a train—should exert more influence on how you write about their sexual encounter than should any anatomical details.

I explain and illustrate many of these ideas in two chapters of basic principles that should apply to almost every kind of sexual encounter or relationship you are moved to write about. In other chapters, I delve into five types of sexual relationships (first times, married people, casual lovers, etc.) and use examples from contemporary fiction that illustrate particular principles, so that you can apply them to your own work. I use contemporary examples rather than historic because there are such profound differences between them, in directness, attitudes and idioms. The older examples often seem archaic and not easily translatable to these times. I use as many examples as I can to suggest the variety of possibilities, but also to teach you to read more deeply and closely, for two vital reasons: so you can ultimately read your own work as critically as you read someone else's, and so you can study *any* sex scene from here on out and absorb its lessons as you need them.

An English professor I knew was very bothered by the word "sex." "It's so vague," she said. "It could mean intercourse, it could mean petting, it could mean anything." For the purposes of this book, for those of you similarly bothered, I want to adopt the definition Fiona Pitt-Kethley put forward in *The Literary Companion to Sex*, which she edited in 1992: "In the end it is perhaps easiest to define sex as anything that can end in orgasm—if you're lucky, that is." Embracing that definition, we will be looking at examples involving heterosexuals, gays, lesbians and, yes, masturbation.

I chose the examples for a variety of literary and nonliterary reasons: quality, length, clarity, and their ability to make sense in excerpted form with a minimum of explanation. I could not use dozens of truly wonderful passages because they were too long or did not deliver all their goods out of context. I do not mean for the selections I have made to stand as the only approved ways to write about sex in fiction, or the only styles in which to write about sex. Like a sex manual, this book is meant to float ideas you may not have considered and give you permission to indulge them. Unlike a set of instructions for building a submarine, these ideas do not have to be strictly adhered to, inch for inch, in order to be of use to you.

Writing well about sex is more than an aesthetic and technical challenge. Because the subject inspires such a dizzying array of emotions, I include a chapter on the personal and social costs of writing explicitly sexual material drawn from interviews I conducted with writers who have taken this path, and several others whose characters prefer to make love in the white spaces between chapters. Excerpts from the interviews also appear throughout the book.

I have devoted a chapter to the issue of writing about sex in the age of AIDS.

Those who make it to the end of the book will be rewarded with the exercises in the last chapter. If you rush ahead to do the exercises before reading the rest of the book, you might find your prose a bit thinner than those who stay the course.

A few words about what this book is not.

The Joy of Writing Sex is not a manifesto meant to encourage writers to compose longer, more frequent or more explicit sex scenes. As in all good writing, quality, not quantity, is what matters. And particularly when writing about sex, a little usually—though not always—goes a long way.

Nor does the book pass moral judgments on specific sexual acts or arrangements, on the fictional characters who engage in them, or the writers who depict them. The writer's job is not to condemn his characters but to portray them in all their supreme complexity. The only sin I recognize is bad writing: prose that is imprecise, flabby, sentimental, and fundamentally dishonest about the experience of being human.

The Joy of Writing Sex is not an encyclopedia of sexual tastes and habits from A to Z. The variety of human sexual experience is too vast to be included in a book meant to help writers sharpen their prose and their literary faculties. You will notice, sooner or later, that I do not offer a single hint on writing about sex with animals or sex on the Internet. I am not saying these are unthinkable, unimaginable, or beyond the realm of literature (see Stanley Elkin's novella, *The Making of Ashburham,* in which a man makes love to and falls in love with a bear, and Ted Mooney's novel, *Easy Travel to Other Planets,* ditto a woman and a dolphin), but my focus throughout this book is on the nature of the relationship between sex partners, and it is beyond my own limited imagination and experience to offer any generally applicable insights as to how a cow or a computer would respond to even the most ardent advances. In his classic book on writing, *Aspects of the Novel,* E.M. Forster shows a similar failure of imagination in leaving animals out of the discussion of actors in a work of fiction. "Other animals have been introduced," he says, "but with limited success, for we know too little so far about their psychology."

Readers will also not find guidance for writing about rape and other forms of sex-related violence. I had intended to include such a chapter, but when I sat down to write it, I realized that the subject was violence, not sex, and the relationship between partners was between a criminal and his or her victim. To be sure, there is plenty to say on this subject, but I was soon convinced that *The Joy of Writing Sex* is not the place to say it.

Though *The Joy of Writing Sex* is also not intended to free you to give voice to your sexual fantasies, desires, traumas or troubles, do not let the principles and exhortations about good writing inhibit you from delving into your personal material in whatever way feels necessary, whether or not the writing ever becomes fiction. In my interview with her, novelist and short story writer Dorothy Allison emphasized the importance of this freedom to write:

> If I hadn't learned to write about sex and particularly to write about my own sexual desires, I don't think I would have survived. I think the guilt, the terror I grew up with was so

extraordinarily powerful if I had not written my way out of it,
I'd be dead. . . . And I think it's vital [to write about], aside
from whether it ever becomes good fiction, particularly for
women with transgressive sexuality . . . [or] people who in
any way feel that their own sexuality cannot be expressed.
Writing can be a way to find a way to be real and sane in the
world, even if it feels a little crazy while you're doing it.

In almost every discussion I've had about *The Joy of Writing Sex*, I'm
asked: Who does it best? My personal favorite is James Salter, who
writes with extraordinary elegance and compresion about sex and
everything else. I would take a page of his from *A Sport and a Pastime*
over a shelf of Anaïs Nin. In a letter to me, John Updike recently
wrote that he doesn't enjoy the sex scenes of other writers as much
as he enjoys his own. I would have to say that some of my own are
my favorites too. Where I thought they were illustrative, I have
included them in this book. But the broader answer to the question
is that I have been on the lookout here, not for The Best Sexy Writer
Around, but for sex scenes and descriptions that engage us aestheti-
cally and emotionally, that bring us deeper into the story, more pal-
pably into the lives of the characters, that strike the right tone and
appear at precisely the right moment. Rosellen Brown is not someone
whose books are chocked with steamy sex, but the bedroom scene in
her recent novel *Before and After* will stay with me, not because the
sex she describes makes the earth move or because the description
of it is lapidary, but because the setting and dialogue leading up to
and following it are so believable and wrenching, because they reveal
so much to us about these characters at a time of crisis, and ultimately,
so much to us about ourselves.

CHAPTER ONE

What Will My Grandmother Think?

Talking to Writers About Sex

"There is no safety in writing well."

—Dorothy Allison (in an interview for this book)

I owe the idea for this chapter of interviews with writers to my late grandmother for her unvarnished reaction to my first novel, *Slow Dancing*. Its opening line went like this: "As Lexi Steiner walked down the hallway of the federal court building in San Diego, she decided that sleeping with men you didn't care about was an acquired taste and that she had acquired it." The story had its raunchy moments, though it also had what I thought was a happyish, girl-gets-nice-guy ending (OK, she's pregnant and they're not married), given where it began. My grandmother did not see it that way. She rarely telephoned me, so I was startled to hear her voice that night. "I just finished your book," she announced, "and I am *not* impressed. This book you're writing now, is *this* going to be a book your grandmother will like?"

She was too frail to read the next novel and did not live to read the third. But her bald statements about the first led me to sense a need for a chapter about how we handle the internal and external censors in our writing lives, now that paid censors have been forced into new lines of work. (A lively history of literary censorship told by banned authors, their publishers, and lawyers who defended them is *Girls Lean Back Everywhere* by Edward DeGrazia.)

My thought was to put this question to a few writers who have written sex scenes of notable excellence. I wanted to be sure to talk to straight and gay writers, to writers of different generations, and, in something of a twist, to a few writers who have chosen *not* to write explicitly about sex while nevertheless delving into the nature and operation of romantic relationships. Reading over interviews with Dorothy Allison, Alan Hollinghurst and Joseph Olshan, who have written explicitly about gay and lesbian sexual relationships and, in Allison's case, childhood incest, I see clearly that they come to write about sex and sexuality from a vastly different set of personal and cultural struggles than do heterosexual writers who came of age in the 1960s and early 1970s. Compared to the straight writers in this small sample, these gay and lesbian writers talk much more about their lack of historic role models in writing about sex and about their sense of purpose, and sometimes shame, in telling outsiders things we do not know about their culture, whether it's the community of incest survivors, promiscuous gay men before AIDS, or gay men who long for love and commitment here and now.

Though I started out with grandmothers on my mind, the arsenal of questions quickly grew as writers gave unexpected answers to my sometimes too-guarded inquiries. In a letter to John Updike, pre-eminent critic and author of some thirty often very sexually explicit novels, short story and poetry collections, I quite primly asked, "Are there writers whose sex scenes you feel do as much for character development as your scenes do?" He wrote back, "Writing my sex scenes physically excites me, as it should. I don't enjoy other writers' as much as my own, but Iris Murdoch in *The Sacred and Profane Love Machine* does bravely try to show sexual compatibility and passion in an otherwise incompatible couple." From then on I got a little nosier with the writers I interviewed and asked them whether their own work aroused them.

I do not have room to publish each interview and letter I received in its entirety. Instead, to paraphrase Bob Dylan, I have tried to synthesize and categorize, in an attempt to squeeze as many voices into this space as I could. Bits of the interviews also appear throughout the book, wherever they seemed to help make a point. In the case of novelist and Sarah Lawrence writing professor Jerome Badanes, I have made an exception and offer separate highlights of our inter-view—a discussion of why he rejected the doctrine "less is more" in writing about sex—at the end of the chapter because he died unexpectedly four days after we spoke. His one novel, a brave and brilliant work, *The Final Opus of Leon Solomon*, was published to much acclaim in 1989 by Alfred A. Knopf, won the Edward Lewis Wallant Award for Best Jewish Novel of the Year, but as of this writing is no longer in print. His second, *Change or Die*, was unfinished at the time of his death.

I conducted interviews by phone or in person with Dorothy Allison, Russell Banks, John Casey, Jane DeLynn, Janice Eidus, Deborah Eisenberg, Stephen McCauley and Joseph Olshan. Alan Hollinghurst, Carol Shields and John Updike were kind enough to reply in writing to my letters.

Question: Who are your censors and how do you silence them? Answer: Just do it.

Canadian writer Robertson Davies was a dutiful son. He said publicly that he waited until his parents were dead to publish his "important fiction." His mother died in 1948, three years before he published his first novel; his father died in 1967, three years before *Fifth Business* appeared, the first of the novels in the celebrated *Deptford Trilogy*, which put Davies on the international literary map. In the spring of 1995, radio interviewer Terry Gross, the host of the nationally syndicated *Fresh Air*, asked him what he feared his parents would have objected to in his work. "It would have embarrassed them," he said simply, "I think because of my attitudes towards a great many things, including sex. I didn't want to distress them, so I didn't write about that kind of thing in the way I eventually did until after they were no longer here."

None of the writers I interviewed took such drastic measures, though novelist Jane DeLynn made a preemptive strike and silenced her censors at the source when she published her fourth novel, *Don Juan in the Village*, a bold, urgent account of a lonely lesbian's sexual adventures over the last few decades. Though DeLynn had written about sex in her fiction before, this novel had, in her words, "much more sex and much more variety."

Jane DeLynn: My father is now dead, though he was alive at the time the book came out. I very easily got him to promise not to read it because I had published an essay having nothing to do with sex, about the Holocaust. It was a personal essay and it had touched on my parents, and he was really angry about that, much more so than my mother. He was very happy to agree not to read it if I suggested it might disturb him. My mother was harder to persuade but I eventually made her promise. She wouldn't promise not to read it but I said, "If you read it, we're just not going to talk about it. You have to promise you're not going to get mad at me if you read it, because you're forewarned." And she did agree.

I don't really find writing about sex necessarily more intimate than writing about other subjects. [In writing *Don Juan*] I had a kind of distanced attitude towards even experiences that might be similar to what I've gone through. I really think that writing about sex is writing about the mind. Once the book was sold, I began to worry about my parents, but I can't say that was much of a consideration. And lovers I didn't worry about at all.

Though Dorothy Allison's short fiction and essays had been known for many years to those who follow lesbian writing, it was not until she published her first novel, *Bastard Out of Carolina*, in 1992, about a poor Southern girl brutalized by her stepfather's incest and beatings, that Allison reached a wider audience. In addition to the literary acclaim the novel brought her, she has found herself a role model for lesbians, incest survivors, and others with what she calls "transgressive sexuality . . . people who in any way feel that their own sexuality cannot be expressed." Over the years she has "been trying to encourage the creation of women's sexual literature," she told me, through her support of new magazines and teaching writing workshops.

Dorothy Allison: My family does not include people who read or . . . the only thing [they] read is popular magazines, self-help books and mysteries. . . . In their mind to write at all is so scary that I didn't have to be afraid of shocking them by writing anything sexually explicit or revealing the fact that I'm a lesbian or even talking about incest. . . . So my family was not the fear. . . . [My fear] was the good girls. . . . I was scared of that middle-class female to whom I have been on occasion sexually attracted and who always seemed like a strange and exotic creature to me, and I was afraid she would think I was [a] demented, evil creature. . . . The other category of good girl was good feminist. Feminism gave me an enormous amount of authority to write about sex and class and my own life at the same time as it set up some really rigid barriers about *how* I could write about it. It was very difficult to write the sections of *Bastard* in which [the narrator] Bone is clearly having profoundly masochistic sexual fantasies. Most of my feminist ideology told me either I was not to talk about that or I was supposed to construct it so that you saw immediately that this was not the child's desire, it was the thing handed to her. It was entirely induced by the sexual assaults by her stepfather and that it didn't have any connection to anything else, which isn't true—the victim ideology that says this isn't something that comes out of you, or that it's anything to deal with. . . .

Keep in mind that *Bastard* was published when I was forty-three. I had been writing for twenty years before I managed to finish that novel. It took a long time to stop those voices and write past them.

I don't think the voices have quieted down. I can keep them under control sometimes! Essentially I think that the last decade gave me some tools. One was other women writers who were trying to do some of the same kind of things I wanted to do. Basically I wanted to write about sexuality and the construction of sexual desire in a very complicated forthright manner, and there were some other writers who were doing that. I think my friendship with writers Joan Nestle and Pat Califia helped a lot. They are two polar opposites. Both are trying to examine sexual desire as an outlaw. Joan is one of the people who organizes the Lesbian Herstory Archives in New York. [Pat Califia is the author of *Macho Sluts* and *Sapphistry.*] In my mind, Joan was more respectable than I was. Pat was more of an outlaw. I could be in this dancing place kind of in the middle.

Joseph Olshan, author of five novels, including *Clara's Heart* and, most recently, *Nightswimmer,* an erotically charged journey through gay New York in the 1990s, admits that he had to "trick" himself into writing explicity in his latest novel. "When you were writing the sex scenes in *Nightswimmer,*" I asked him, "was it straightforward or did you have to dig deep?"

Joseph Olshan: I had to dig deep. I had to kind of trick myself. I had this feeling that the richest material that one has as a writer is the part that one has to trick oneself into writing, because in a way it's what the psyche guards against. Your best stories, your best material, your most lyrical lines are the ones hardest to get to because there's something in you that doesn't want that to come out, that doesn't want that to be exposed. You know when the body goes into shock when you get hurt, it's the same kind of thing. You've got to really wake yourself up in a way, to get to that part. If I thought about all the people who were going to read the scenes when I sat down to write them, I probably wouldn't do it. . . .

[Yet] I think I am one person who should probably be writing about sex. It seems to come naturally to me. It's something I think a lot about. Not the act of sex but the dynamics of the relationship and what it means. And love and loneliness and obsession. . . . When I think about the sex scenes in *Nightswimmer* . . . reaching orgasm is not the important thing. . . . Very few of the sex scenes actually reach orgasm. It's the connection, it's how people finally connect when they get into the rhythm of making love. Once that happens it's not as interesting. . . . But it's fascinating for the outside world to see how the two heavenly bodies dock, become synchronized.

Writers are not the only ones in this relationship between writer and reader who rely on tricks to help them through the difficult passages. Russell Banks, author of some dozen works of fiction, including the novels *Continental Drift*, *The Sweet Hereafter* and, most recently, *Rule of the Bone*, told me that he has never censored himself when writing about sexual matters, partly, he thinks, because of a freedom his mother gave him years ago, when his second novel was published.

Russell Banks: My mother is a born-again Christian. I love her and admire her and am very close to her. She's fastidious about language. My second novel has some pretty bizarro sex scenes. They're comic in a way. They're very broad and reckless. It's not realistic fiction at all. My mother told me she had read the book. I said, "But what about all those dirty parts, Mom?" She said, "As soon as I hear them coming, I jump ahead." I talked to her recently about them and she says she still does it that way. She says, "As soon as I spot them coming, I just jump ahead."

British novelist Alan Hollinghurst, whose first novel, *The Swimming Pool Library*, has the stature of a contemporary gay classic, characterizes his descriptions of gay sex in that novel as "unapologetic." His answer, in writing, to my question about internal and external censors was refreshingly uncomplicated.

Alan Hollinghurst: I did not have to overcome any reluctance to write sex scenes. I was apprehensive about how my parents would react to the book, but after initial disconcertment they became interested in it, and in its success.

Whether we already possess or still need to cultivate Hollinghurst's unself-conscious approach to the subject, it is useful to keep John Casey's advice—suitable for framing—in mind. Casey is the author of the novels *Spartina*, which won the National Book Award, and *An American Romance*, which a friend of mine described as "Henry James with sex."

John Casey: There is a potency [in writing explicitly about sex] you have to be careful of, because it can disrupt the reader's experience of reading the book. But you *can't* think about the reader—any reader—over your shoulder when you're writing. You can go back later and you can worry about people's qualms. When you're alone in your working room, you can't think about anyone.

Question: What's hot and what's not?
Answer: You would be surprised.

When I first began asking writers what books they found arousing or had when they were young, it was to educate myself. I assumed I would end up with a reading list of the smartest sexy books around—everything, I guessed, from Gustave Flaubert's *Madame Bovary* to Terry Southern's comic *Candy*. But most of the answers I got early in the process were so unexpected, I gave up all hope of amassing an erotic reading list and kept asking the question anyway—because the answers said so much about the quirky and uncategorizable nature of human sexuality. My sense I was onto something interesting began with John Casey telling me that two of the most memorable sexy novels of his youth were Stendhal's *The Charterhouse of Parma* and *The Red and the Black*. When he reread *The Charterhouse of Parma* years later, he was astonished to see there was much less passion in the scenes between Fabrizio and his aunt than he had remembered as an adolescent. "As a teenager with raging hormones you keep adding stuff to what's really there," he explains. In writing his own much more explicit sex scenes, what's important to him are not the mechanics but "the swoon. The delicious palpitations of one's heart is the real eroticism."

When I reported some of the early book titles to Jane DeLynn, she observed that what makes a memorable sexy book for many of us is "obviously in the realm of the mind." She confessed that for her "the sexiest scene in literature" occurs in Virginia Woolf's novel, *Mrs. Dalloway*, which concerns the middle-aged Clarissa Dalloway, whose husband, a Member of Parliament, recently insisted she sleep alone in their attic, in a narrow bed, to help recover from an illness. As she fixes up the ascetic room and prepares for a big party she is giving that night, she thinks about "this question of love, . . . this falling in love with women," and of her bold, sexually aware childhood friend Sally Seton, who kissed her once on the lips when they were nineteen. They had been walking on the terrace with other visitors to the house. "Then came the most exquisite moment of her whole life passing a stone urn with flowers in it. Sally stopped; picked a flower; kissed her on the lips. The whole world might have turned upside down!"

John Updike gave a reading list closer to the one I expected from other writers, which segues nicely into his thematic summaries of his own work.

John Updike: Joyce and Lawrence, of course, as models of novelists who took sex in stride in their representations of life; but also Edmund Wilson's *Memoirs of Hecate County* and the novels of Erskine Caldwell and James M. Cain, who, within the bounds of [19]30s-40s possibility, wrote about sex in a way that made a strong impression on an adolescent boy. And Norman Mailer's ground-breaking story of 1958, "The Time of Her Time," which I read with astonishment while standing in a bookstore. After 1961 and Henry Miller and Grove Press, the frontier challenge was replaced by a need to farm the opened-up territory with real and interesting accounts of sex lives as part of lives. *Couples*, for instance, was about an illicit couple bonding through fellatio. *A Month of Sundays* tried to show impotence as an effect of moral scruple. In *Rabbit is Rich*, married love is played for a certain comedy, and [in] the scene with Thelma and Rabbit, buggery and water games are presented rather tenderly, as attempts, in a sex-saturated world, to make an impression and live up to the surrounding porn culture. Pornography and theology in *Roger's Version* are seen as kindred mental exercises, both delicious.

For Carol Shields, an American-born Canadian writer whose novel, *The Stone Diaries*, won the Pulitzer Prize in 1995, a scene in a short story by Alice Munro, "Bardon Bus," is her favorite erotic encounter in print. Shields is a wickedly astute chronicler of the quirks and longings of ordinary people who turn out not to be so ordinary, a sort of Jane Austen with sex.

Carol Shields: The most erotic scene I've ever witnessed was my uncle bending over at the dining room table to kiss the back of my aunt's neck. It was summer time and she was wearing a sundress and just lifting a spoonful of sherbet to her lips. They were middle-aged then. I was a child, maybe nine or ten. But I recognized "it." I thought I might try to write about this experience. But all the old problems occur—how to make such a small gesture *felt*.

The work of novelist and award-winning short story writer Janice Eidus is often set in New York City and steeped in classic myths retold about contemporary urban life. For example, "Ladies with Long Hair" was inspired by the death from AIDS of Eidus' hairdresser. In the *Lysistrata*-based story, women whose hairdressers have all died of AIDS become politicized; they refuse to cut their hair again until a cure is found, and with their long, long locks, they stage protests and demonstrations.

Janice Eidus: When I was about twelve I read *Romeo and Juliet* and I thought it was *just* the most erotic thing on earth, and when I started thinking about other books that have mattered to me in terms of erotic arousal or passion, I realize that there are certain kinds of scenes that *Romeo and Juliet* has that are always in these other books . . . an obsessive desire that's unleashed in both the women and the men, not an unrequited passion. *Adele H.* [the story of Victor Hugo's daughter's obsessive fixation on a man who is indifferent to her] is not quite as erotic to me as when both are really touched in this way, when there's a defiance of convention—the forbidden that's good and ethical, because I'm really such a humanist. One of the things I find unerotic in fiction, and a lot of contemporary fiction has it, is nihilism, people who defy convention but in a very bloodless, cold-blooded way. . . . Do you know Angela Carter's writing? I love all her novels. A few I read when I discovered her ten years ago I thought were incredibly erotic. They use a kind of mythology and sexuality combined. There's something almost beautiful about using these age-old myths and reinventing them in a contemporary sexualized context. . . . You know the archetypes and they very often follow the kind of defiance of convention and tremendous risk in the name of a very positive desire in love.

In a slightly different form, I put the sexy book question to Alan Hollinghurst. Had there been particular books and authors he felt had given him permission to write about his characters' sex lives?

Alan Hollinghurst: I suppose like anyone, but particularly perhaps like any gay person with literary inclinations, I tried to find accounts of gay sexual experiences in books, but of course in the best authors the sex scenes were often deeply colored by some other preoccupation—e.g., in Genet or Burroughs. I always found those "scandalous" sex books of the '50s and '60s, posing as exposés or as a kind of social anthropology or as somehow "medical," to be terribly depressing. I had done work as a graduate student on earlier gay writers—specifically E.M. Forster, Ronald Firbank and L.P. Hartley—who hadn't been able to write openly about their sexuality, but had created fascinating opportunities for expressing it in oblique or coded forms. And then there were the—generally very routine and fantastic—stories in porno magazines. It's hard to think back to intentions of ten years ago or more [when he was writing *Swimming Pool*]; but I do remember feeling that the segregation of experience into the Forsterian cryptic and the baldly pornographic did some deep violence to the way life was actually lived and felt, where sexual thoughts and deeds—especially in the case of a beautiful and promiscuous young gay man, as in *The Swimming Pool Library*—were intimately wrapped up with everything else in life. Hardly anyone writing literary novels about gay life, it seemed to me, had really been prepared to mix the sex in in this essentially realistic way; there was a bit in [Edmund White's] *A Boy's Own Story*, but *The Beautiful Room is Empty*, which has far more sex in it, had not yet come out. I agree with Edmund White that it felt like quite a novel thing to be doing at that time. So no, I don't think there were other authors who gave me permission to write about my characters' sex lives in the way I did.

17

Question: Does your own work turn you on?
Answer: Not always.
Dorothy Allison: No, not by the time it's finished! In the early stages, yes, sometimes, but not by the time I've worked it down and gotten it in publishable form.

Alan Hollinghurst: No, I'm not physically excited by writing about sex; the point for me has always been to write about it with as steady an eye as I try to bring to bear on everything else. So much sex writing goes wrong. . . . Anyway, much of the sex I describe [in *The Swimming Pool Library* and *The Folding Star*] is not great sex; it's fleeting, or absurd, or unhappy or unsatisfactory in some way.

For many writers and readers, the sexiest writing operates on the metonymy principle, which John Casey describes this way: "If you have one thing stand for another, it tends to heighten all the things that aren't being talked about." For many writers and readers, suggestion, suppression and sublimation are more potent aphrodisiacs than the real thing. Carol Shields reported that she wrote an academic paper several years ago about

> Jane Austen's use (non-use really) of body parts in her books. (Fortunately there is a concordance available.) There are something like two ankles and one nose in all those books. Also three breasts, but all belonging to men. And so the rise on the erotic thermometer is signalled obliquely, a flutter of a hand standing in for a major sexual response—all of it on this curious miniaturized scale, like looking into the doll house of sensuality.

When I interviewed Stephen McCauley, whose three novels, *The Man of the House*, *The Easy Way Out*, and *The Object of My Affection* are contemporary comedies of manners that focus on gay relationships, we talked a lot about the power of metonymy in *Lolita* and *Madame Bovary* and about his own reasons for not going into sexual detail in his own fiction.

Stephen McCauley: *Madame Bovary*, for example, is filled with lush, sensual descriptions that heighten the reader's awareness of the erotic tension between the characters. The way Flaubert describes the texture of soot on a fireplace or the sound of water falling on a silk parasol or the look of Emma's tongue licking the bottom of a glass of liqueur conveys a powerful sense of sublimated sexuality. Flaubert's attention to all the senses is so exact and exquisite, he can write a powerful erotic scene with no physical contact. I suppose it helps to be a genius.

Sex scenes invariably fall flat when the urge to titillate or, worse still, to be titillated, overpowers a writer's attention to his or her characters. Like all scenes in fiction, a sex scene should be specific and deepen the reader's understanding of the characters. You can't do that if you lapse into an all-purpose, porn-inspired vocabulary for describing sex.

When my first novel, *The Object of My Affection*, was published, it received some criticism in the gay press because it contained no explicit sex scenes. The attitude seemed to be that the book was unliberated or politically regressive because of that. But the narrator is extremely diffident. It would have been out of character for him to describe his sex life in detail—except for a few broad complaints—though there was no doubt in my mind that he was comfortable with his homosexuality. I convinced myself that there was something subversive in opting for no explicit sex. Of course, I'm open to the possibility that I'm just shy and repressed.

As a writer, you always want to lure your readers into the world of the book and keep them deeply immersed. With a certain kind of generically titillating sex scene, you run the risk of losing them completely, of sending them off into their own masturbatory fantasies rather than paying attention to what's going on in the novel.

Deborah Eisenberg, whose short stories have been published over the last fifteen years in *The New Yorker* and gathered in two collections, *Transactions in a Foreign Currency* and *Under the 82nd Airborne*, also decided that the explicit sex route was not for her. Her insights about the limitations of writing explicitly about sex also serve as advice to those who take sex on: Be specific.

Deborah Eisenberg: I don't really feel that there are special problems involved in writing about sex—I mean, in writing directly and graphically about sex—but I think maybe the same problems that are involved in writing about anything are likely to be exaggerated. The anatomical possibilities are limited, so a poorly written sex scene can be a little like hearing an eight-year-old describe the plot of his favorite movie. And on the other hand, because every reader brings to every sex scene *vivid* prior experience, writing graphically about sex can also be a little like writing: *Dead mother.* You'll get a response, all right, but it might not be the response you want, or the response that proceeds from all the careful work you've done to show exactly what's happening between these two particular people—or these twelve particular people—right now. The hazard is that if you, the writer, are insufficiently in control, the response you'll get is the one that the reader would have had to any sex scene whatsoever that came his or her way. The problems of cliché and generality, which are exactly what writing is a battle against, are especially hard to outwit when you're writing about sex because the reader's response is so likely to be automatic and blinding. It's as if a flash were going off, obscuring all the specifics and detail and nuance you've constructed so carefully about your characters and their encounter. Of course, that's the way sex sometimes works in real life—you know: Well, I actually don't happen to care just now *who* that person is—and if that's what you want, fine.

I haven't really written that often, I suppose, directly about sex. Who knows what I'll feel like doing in the future, but up till now, it seems I've been somewhat more interested in the thwarted impulse, or something of the sort—the erotic charge inappropriately pervading all sorts of experience. And to me—well, there's all of *Madame Bovary*, of course, but one of the most sexually interesting *scenes* in literature is in *Anna Karenina* when Vronsky returns to his barracks after seeing Anna, and his roommate tells him an absolutely idiotic, very funny anecdote about helmets. Anna isn't in the scene at all—she's far away—but you're very aware of her. And the uncanny giddiness you experience along with Vronsky has to do, I think, with the shift in sexual power between Anna and him at that moment; the erotic obsession is like an animal that's released Vronsky temporarily, to settle its entire weight on Anna. The sexuality that's collapsed into that scene with the roommate is just so complex—and intense, and accurate, and *specific.*

OVER THE TOP: EXCERPTS FROM AN INTERVIEW WITH JEROME BADANES.

The narrator of Jerome Badanes' masterful novel, *The Final Opus of Leon Solomon*, an Auschwitz survivor and scholar of Jewish history, is about to commit suicide after being caught stealing papers from the

New York Public Library. As he prepares to die, he writes his final opus on a stack of yellow legal pads, the story of his life. The novel includes many graphic sex scenes between people normally forbidden from intimate contact: Solomon and his sister, two Jews trying to pass for Aryans in occupied Warsaw; and four decades later, Solomon and the daughter of a Gestapo officer.

Elizabeth Benedict: The sex scenes in *The Final Opus of Leon Solomon* go against the advice we generally give people in writing about sex, that less is more. What made you take it so far over the top?

Jerome Badanes: First of all I don't write about sex at all. I mean, I have sex in my book but I'm not sitting down to write sex. I'm sitting down to write something else. The sex is a vehicle to get to that other place. What I'm always trying to get to in my books is the ability of human beings to connect regardless of circumstances. So when I have my survivor have an affair with the daughter of a Nazi, they were trying to get past that history and they failed to. I made it as graphic as I did because I wanted the reader to experience with them both the desperation and the wonderousness of their attempt to get past it. I wanted the reader to be there through every detail, and I consider all those sexual details sacred. They're not smutty, they're not dirty, they're what people do. I wanted the reader to experience that, to feel them feeling the thrill of connection and the despair of knowing that the connection will be broken, that it can't be a lasting connection.

In the scenes with my main character when he's a young man and his sister that are on the edge of being totally incestuous, except they don't have intercourse, I wanted to get the reader close to it because I saw those scenes themselves as I said in the book as a Kaddish for their lost youth and for their fate as Jews in Europe in occupied Warsaw. The Warsaw ghetto was just a few blocks away. . . . And to have the reader experience that Kaddish you had to go through the details. It's fine for the writers who just want to suggest things but I felt I wanted to take the reader right there and take them to a place that is maybe awkward for them or embarrasses them or makes them nervous but take them and keep pushing at it until the reader comes to that other place, and they feel what they felt. I don't believe in minimalization.

Benedict: You mean because you're dealing with something as disturbing as incest, the reader can say yes, in that situation I might have done that?

Badanes: In some sense the moral imperative was for them to connect, both of them doomed, the sister totally doomed, the brother knowing that because of her rheumatoid arthritis. I want them to experience the degradation of having to go through all the taboo feelings, so I decided that instead of suggesting, I would say in detail what they did. Not using anything but descriptive language. . . . A reviewer talked about the sex, said that in a world turned upside down, the moral moment might include something as taboo-laden as incest. It's a comment on the world turned upside down. A comment on history. All the sex in *The Final Opus* is in dire settings, deathly settings, as a way of remembering and being a moment of life in a death world, a way of creating a moment of good faith in a world filled with bad faith. . . .

Though I understood that and I felt that as the larger ambition, . . . I wanted to make sure that it was sexy, so that the reader could experience it, and one way to make sure it's sexy—the first way—is to make sure I find it sexy. I wanted to feel sexy as I was writing about sex in even the most dangerous or tragic or historically horrifying circumstances, and that can make you feel a little bad, because you're feeling sexy about something horrible, but of course I wanted the reader to feel that too. That itself is a paradox. And that's how the characters feel. And that was my way of doing that, so, I tried to write sex scenes in such a way that the reader found them sexy, both men readers and women readers, and I was only hoping women readers, because I'm not a woman, but I could imagine myself into womanness in the scenes.

That was my goal. That's not easy to do. So that's why I couldn't do less is more. I wanted to really soak the reader in the details of sex so they could feel everything, so they could feel the paradox of it, sex while everyone's dying around them or they're about to be killed or they're breaking taboos. I wanted them to feel all that stuff, and I needed a lot of detail to do that. So that's why it's over the top, except I don't think it's over the top. I think it has to be over the top to be in the right place.

The Iliad graphically describes the killing of people. Not only the killing but the humiliation that people feel when they're totally at the mercy of the person who's about to kill them, and they're begging for their lives and they get murdered anyway, the way Achilles kills Hector. You get it from moment to moment. We can be very graphic about violence but to be graphic about sex is a more complicated thing apparently. Society has more trouble taking it. Actually, being that graphic about violence made the violence transcendent, it made you think about it, made you suddenly feel. When we see films of people getting shot we don't get a chance to feel what it is to be a person in the few seconds before death, totally at the mercy of the other person, someone who has totally lost his or her own will, totally enslaved at that moment before death. Homer gives that to us in some way, that modern thing that's been dumped. What I tried to do with the sex in *The Final Opus* was what I see being done with violence in *The Iliad*—deliver the moment in some way.

CHAPTER TWO

A Sex Scene Is
Not a Sex Manual

Ten Basic Principles

"Sex is something I really don't understand too hot. You never know where *the hell you are. I keep making up these sex rules for myself, and then I break them right away."*

—J.D. Salinger, *The Catcher in the Rye*

In the best fiction writing about sex, even if it is a brief paragraph, we come to the end knowing not just "what happened" but something about the characters, their sensibilities, circumstances or inner lives, about the narrator who is relating the events, the concerns of the author—or all of the above. A well-written sex scene engages us on many levels: erotic, aesthetic, psychological, metaphorical, even philosophical.

Yet when reading a novel or short story whose sex scenes hook us on all these levels, we are most often so fully in its thrall that we don't analyze and compartmentalize our reactions; we just keep reading and enjoying. But as we set out to learn to write a good scene, like an apprentice auto mechanic, we need to study what's under the hood and find out how to take the engine apart, before we learn how to put it back together.

As you embark on this endeavor, take a lesson Holden Caulfield had a hard time learning in *The Catcher in the Rye*: Don't even *think* about rules. There are no secret formulas, no shortcuts, no clever tricks to writing a good sex scene. Sex and fiction are much too particular, too personal—too unorganizable—to reduce them to a simple list of dos and don'ts. I offer instead, as John Gardner does in his informal textbook, *The Art of Fiction: Notes on Craft for Young Writers*, what he calls "general principles" that are broad enough to accommodate most every sexual appetite and literary style.

But before we get to those, let's look at three primary reasons why it can be so difficult to write well about sex in fiction:

1. Thirty-five years ago, explicit sex scenes in fiction were rare. Today they are as plentiful as pennies and, many would argue, about as valuable. When everything has already been said ad nauseam, how can we hope to make an original contribution?

2. Sex seems simple but it isn't. Or, as E.M. Forster said in his classic treatise on writing fiction, *Aspects of the Novel*, "When human beings love they try to get something. They also try to give something, and this double aim makes love more complicated than food or sleep. It is selfish and altruistic at the same time, and no amount of specialization in one direction quite atrophies the other."

The mechanics *are* simple, but the politics and psychodynamics— its hidden messages and meanings—make it the most complex of human exchanges. And despite sex saturation in the culture and sex education on TV, everything we need to know about our personal sexuality we must learn in the privacy of our own lives.

What makes sex so powerful an urge is our desire to connect with another human being. But as soon as you involve that other person— the Other—the equation is no longer simple. You long for an unfamiliar heartbeat against your skin but what you often get is someone else's heartache, someone colder and more distant than the warm body you sought, or someone as fragile and needy as you are. (Never, Nelson Algren cautions us, "sleep with someone whose troubles are worse than your own.") The costs of sexual intimacy can be exorbitant.

3. Sex means something different to each of us, and its meanings can multiply and change from minute to minute, and evolve over time, as people and their cultures change. Sex can be an expression of affection, love, fear, vulnerability, anger, power, rage, submission—or nearly all of these at once. Sex strips us of our defenses, leaving us vulnerable to feelings that are often repressed.

THE TOP TEN

Writing fiction about sex is no more or less difficult than writing good fiction about anything else: Committing every new word to paper leaves us wondering if we are headed in the right direction and how we will know if we are not. But sex as a subject presents its own thorny challenges. Let's begin with ten general principles to help guide you as you slip between the sheets.

1. A sex scene or description is not a sex manual.
2. A good sex scene does not have to be about good sex.
3. It's OK—really!—to be aroused by your own writing.
4. Your fear is your best friend.
5. Sex is nice but character is destiny.
6. Only your characters know for sure (what to call it).
7. Take your cues from your characters.
8. Your characters must want and want intensely.
9. A good sex scene is always about sex and something else.
10. Who your characters are to each other is key.

Let's look at each of these more closely.

1. A sex scene or description is not a sex manual. Writing about sex in fiction is different from writing about harpooning a whale; it's safe to assume your readers have had a good bit of experience with the former and almost none with the latter. We don't need a thorough report on the hydraulics unless they are relevant to your character's state of mind and your story's larger concerns (see, for example, the discussion of Philip Roth's novel *Portnoy's Complaint* in chapter three). "We know about the physiology," Russell Banks reminds us. "What a writer needs to tell us in a sex scene are the things we don't know."

For instance, we learn a certain character has a passion for pacifiers in this brief passage from *Love in the Time of Cholera*, a rich novel about lifelong love and passion by Colombian-born, Nobel prize-winner Gabriel García Márquez, which, he has said, was inspired by his parents' relationship. In this description, García Márquez says nothing about bodies or body parts, but Sara's pacifier ritual conveys all we need to know about the passionate, playful and unself-conscious nature of her sexual relationship with Florentino. By keeping our eyes on pacifiers rather than on body parts, in a memorable, original fashion, the author reveals information about the lovers (Sara's lack of inhibition, Florentino's pleasure in that) and the culture that sanctions such a relationship. The pacifiers also remind us of sexual passion's power to hurl us back to elemental urges of infancy:

> What Florentino Ariza liked best about her was that in order to reach the heights of glory, she had to suck on an infant's pacifier while they made love. Eventually they had a string of them, in every size, shape, and color they could find in the market, and Sara Noriéga hung them on the headboard so she could reach them without looking in her moments of extreme urgency.

2. A good sex scene does not have to be about good sex. The aim of pornography, whether it's a movie or a magazine, is to arouse the consumer. Or as novelist and critic Cathleen Schine described it in *The New York Review of Books*, "Every pornographic narrative huffs and puffs to the same inexorable conclusion; tab A being fitted breathlessly into slot B. . . . However ornate the preparation, the outcome is inevitable." Coitus interruptus, disappointing sex, lovers who are less than enthusiastic in their coupling, a lover who drops off to sleep before the moment of truth—all would leave purveyors of porn demanding their money back. But in writing a sex scene in a serious piece of fiction, we have the privilege of lavishing our attention on characters who seem to flunk their major subject more often than they pass it. In fiction a sexual connection that goes awry or has cataclysmic consequences is often more interesting than one that leaves the characters sated and deliriously happy.

Sexual encounters are a chance for your characters to make connections or fail to make them. The needier they are to connect, the more interesting their disappointment and its aftermath can be. The shock of dashed expectations can (and perhaps should) lead characters to have insights, even epiphanies, about matters much broader than the condition of their genitals. This is certainly the case in examples I discuss later in the book from Erica Jong's *Fear of Flying* and John Lonie's short story, "Contact."

Perhaps the most interesting literary category of "unsatisfying sex" is sex that satisfies physically but leaves the lovers angry, empty, still yearning, or unequally fulfilled when it's over. See the discussions of *Before and After* and *Slow Dancing*.

3. It's OK—really!—to be aroused by your own writing. If it's good enough for John Updike, it's good enough for the rest of us. "Writing my sex scenes physically excites me, as it should," he said in the letter quoted in chapter one. Jerome Badanes echoes this in discussing the graphic sex scenes in his novel, *The Final Opus of Leon Solomon:* "One way to make sure it's sexy—the first way—is to make sure I find it sexy." This does not mean that a good sex scene is just the writer's let-it-rip sexual fantasy. Far from it. Badanes again: "Sex scenes should not be advertisements for oneself." They should, as we stress in other sections of this book, issue from character, deepen our involvement in the story, and/or fuel the plot. None of that means they can't be arousing too.

4. Your fear is your best friend. When I asked Dorothy Allison what advice she gives students on writing about sex in their fiction, the power of her answer led me to make this a basic principle. Here's what she said:

> I believe that fear is useful. Remember when you played a game when you were a kid and you'd be looking for something and somebody would know where it was and they'd say, You're warm, you're warm, you're hot, you're cold! You've gone the wrong way. The fear works that way. What you are most afraid of is where the energy will flow the strongest, and for a writer, if you write in that direction, toward where the fear is, it's like a homing signal for what you need to do. . . .
>
> There's no safety in writing well. There is no way to be naked, which is what you have to be to be a good writer . . . and still be safe. . . . I think one of the things that's happened in sexual writing is we've gotten the notion that nakedness is about being explicit about details and techniques. I find that really tedious. What is truly naked is emotional exposure. And for every writer that's different. The place where you're pushing yourself the most emotionally is going to be different. It's way different for a lesbian than for a straight woman, it's way different depending on your age and the world you were brought up in, depending on who you're most afraid of, whether it's your family or those middle-class white girls that always made me so convinced they would

spot me and throw me out. Every person has a fear. And your fear is your best friend.

5. Sex is nice but character is destiny. If you are like me, when you think of your favorite books, it is compelling characters, not plots, that come immediately to mind—characters or pairs of characters: Dorothea and Mr. Casaubon from George Eliot's *Middlemarch*; the fifteen-year-old French girl and her Chinese lover from Marguerite Duras' *The Lover*; the deluded narrator of Ford Madox Ford's *The Good Soldier*. Fiction without characters we care about is a dreary place to spend time.

What does this have to do with sex? Everything. We don't have to love your characters or trust them with our children, but if they don't engage us, we won't care even if they get lucky and find someone who wants to go to bed with them.

I need to care about your characters enough to care about their sex lives.

6. Only your characters know for sure (what to call it). This is the part about writing about sex that everyone wants the answer to: What do you call it? When he was writing his first novel, *Body and Soul*, Frank Conroy, the director of the University of Iowa's Writers' Workshop and author of a classic memoir, *Stop-Time*, told me that he dreaded having to write the sex scenes he knew were part of the story: "Do you say 'cock,' do you say 'prick'? Do you use all those words like 'slippery'?" Though I cannot give you a list of *les mots justes*, I offer these general guidelines:

- Call it what your characters would call it. If this happens to be slang that might be unfamiliar to your readers, or slang that sounds cute or out of character, establish that this word or these words are the accepted argot for this couple or in this circle.
- Whatever your choice, make sure it is appropriate to the tone of the book.
- Don't be cute and evasive—unless the characters are and you have established credible reasons for their attitudes.
- There is always the clinical terminology, which may not win any prizes for poetry, but will get you where you need to go without calling too much attention to itself.
- It may not be necessary to call it anything. In his novel,

Paradise News, discussed in chapter three, David Lodge has written a very sexy scene and circumvented any need to name names.

7. Take your cues from your characters. Mickey Friedman, author of seven mystery novels, recently said to me, "It's difficult to pin down what my characters should do when they drift toward the bedroom." Easy. Let your characters show you the way. Follow them into the bedroom, don't make them wait for instructions. If that advice still leaves you stuck in neutral in the living room, gaping at your befuddled couple, ignore one of them for a few minutes and focus all your loving, observant attention on the other. What does she want to happen—in the next ten minutes and in the next ten days? What else or who else does she have on her mind? Is there anything she is afraid of at the moment? If she were asked to describe what the man in her arms wants from her tonight, what would she say? If she were asked what he might want from her tomorrow morning, what would she say?

Once you can locate one character's state of mind and desire, turn your attention to her partner. How does he respond to her stated and unstated fears and needs?

When you decide it's time for your characters to hop into bed together, you may be pushing them to do something they are not ready for or don't want as much as you want them to want it. How will you know? See Principle 8.

8. Your characters must want and want intensely. Whether your characters are moving toward the bedroom or the Eiffel Tower, don't let them go too far without taking stock of *what they want*—in the next ten minutes and as fictional entities in this universe they have helped you create. Novelist Janet Burroway explains this matter of "wanting" as an elemental force in her book, *Writing Fiction.* Her words apply to writing about sex and everything else:

> It is true that in fiction, in order to engage our attention and sympathy, the central character must want and want intensely. The thing that character wants need not be violent or spectacular; it is the intensity of the wanting that counts. She may want only to survive, but if so she must want enormously to survive, and there must be distinct cause to doubt she will succeed.

If you do not know what to do when your characters drift toward the bedroom, learn to recognize this uncertainty as one of nature's warning signs that you need to check in with them, like a doctor making rounds. Begin by making sure at least one character wants something out of the upcoming sexual encounter. But whatever your character wants, remember that in fiction it is always more interesting if he does not get what he wants, if he gets what he wants but finds it was not what he wanted after all, or if he has to pay a heavy price for what he has gotten.

A character who wants something that his partner does not want to give him is what dramatic conflict is all about. Some conflict leads to large-scale strife between characters; some is just verbal bantering that tells us about the nature of your characters' intimacy. And some seemingly innocuous parrying can foreshadow more high stakes drama yet to come. In the realm of writing about sex, dramatic conflict can begin with no more than two characters who have different expectations for an afternoon rendezvous.

9. A good sex scene is always about sex and something else. One of the rules of fiction writing is that the rules are meant to be broken, but here's one I've never found a reason to tamper with: Make sure there are two things happening at once, whether you're writing dialogue or a sex scene. I don't mean there has to be sex and stamp collecting; I mean the sex needs a purpose in your story beyond the momentary frisson it brings your characters. It needs to reveal something about them, act as a metaphor, a symbol, or an illustration of an aspect of your theme, your plot, and/or your characters' desires and dilemmas.

When I asked Russell Banks if there was a point in his career when he felt inhibited writing about sex and a moment when the inhibition lifted, he gave an answer that led to another example of the two-things-at-once principle:

> I don't think I ever felt particularly inhibited about it. I think when I first began writing I was less clear about the difference between writing and fantasizing, and so when I wrote about sex I tended to have a sexual fantasy. It took a while to realize that wasn't doing anyone any good, not even me, and it wasn't doing the writing any good. I began to realize I had to approach it with the same attention to craft

and to function in the larger work that I did with every other scene. . . .

There is a scene in *Continental Drift* when [main character] Bob Dubois is having sex and imagines himself at a boat landing on the shore of the new world skimming up over the beach with the waves forcing him forward, which is meant to be a slight parody of the conventions of sex writing, where they always invoke waves and tides and things like that. And also a slight parody of the unconscious sexist language used to describe "the new world." Since this fit with some of the themes of the book, I thought it was useful to do. And I lost complete contact with whether or not it was good for Bob!— because I was having so much fun relating the sex to all these other things and using it in other ways. At that point I realized what a powerful and wonderful metaphor a sex scene can be in a story, for things utterly other than sex. How you could use a sex scene to develop and dramatize themes in the book that had nothing to do with sex. . . . This was when I began to realize the literary possibilities of a sex scene and didn't just use it either sentimentally or to indulge myself in a sexual fantasy.

Sex in real life doesn't have to be about anything but sex; however, in fiction it has to reveal something about who the characters are, what they want, what they might not get, what they think they can get away with, or what this collision of bodies has to do with everything that comes before and after in your story.

10. Who your characters are to each other is key. Have your literary lovers been married for thirty years? Have they just met? Are they old friends? There is no more important element in crafting a sex scene than the relationship between sex partners. It is so crucial that chapters five through ten are devoted to exploring the nature of specific sexual relationships and how writers can learn to combine the general truths about them with the particular circumstances of their characters and their stories. In the meantime, turn to chapter three for a few more general principles that are beyond the basics.

"Surprise Me" and Other Literary Come-Ons

Beyond the Basics

"The trick is, of course, once sex is not off-limits, to keep it from being boring, and to make it continuous with the book's psychology and symbolism elsewhere."

—John Updike (in his letter to me)

Many of the earlier principles introduced you to the idea of focusing on your characters' whole selves and relationships to one another rather than on their body parts as you feel your way through a sex scene. The principles in this chapter focus on more technical aspects of *how* to make these characters and relationships come alive and do all the things you need them to do for your story—chief among them, keep us from being bored by a sex scene that's all plumbing. These are the principles we will be exploring and learning to apply here:

1. Sex is not an ATM withdrawal. Narrate from inside your characters' bodies and minds, not from a camera set up to record the transaction.
2. Hire a decorator.
3. Your characters don't have to speak to each other but don't forget that they can.
4. You need not be explicit but you must be specific.
5. Surprise me.

1. Sex is not an ATM withdrawal. Narrate from inside your characters' bodies and minds, not from a camera set up to record the transaction. If you are writing about a Peeping Tom, his experience of sex-from-a-distance is exactly what you should be describing. But if your character is plunging headlong into bed with another character or two, put us right there with at least one of them. Whatever else it is, sex is a physical experience, and part of your job is, in some way, to make some of those sensations immediate and accessible to the reader. This does not mean you must file a report on every twitch. Nor does it mean you should limit your observations to the feel of flesh against flesh. In addition to unruly memories and unbidden thoughts, people have eyes, ears and noses, each with a highly specialized and sensitive job to perform. Anaïs Nin described this orchestra of senses in her diary: "There are so many minor senses, all running like tributaries into the mainstream of sex, nourishing it."

To sharpen your awareness of your senses and to discover a language in which to write about them, read Diane Ackerman's sensuous and learned study, *A Natural History of the Senses.* As a poet and dedicated sensualist, she offers a history and appreciation of the senses so rich you may come to believe your nose is the most important part of your body.

2. Hire a decorator. Most of the principles we've looked at have focused on setting the emotional stage, creating characters who are fully developed enough so that we can care about their sex lives along with the rest of their lives, and so that the sex scenes relate to the larger story. But to really deliver the moment, as Jerome Badanes puts it, we also need to see them in their physical surroundings, whether they are in a hammock or the Lincoln Room in the White House. What your characters see around them is as important as what they feel and remember.

Once they begin to disrobe, make them as aware of their physical surroundings as they are when they are not making love. Create a connection between their physical surroundings, their relationship, and the larger concerns of the story. John Casey does this beautifully in his novel *Spartina,* about a Rhode Island fisherman, Dick Pierce, in love with his wife, his lover Elsie, and the fishing boat called *Spartina* that he is determined to build and then has to save heroically when a hurricane threatens to destroy it. In a scene where he and

Elsie make love at night along the banks of a salt marsh, the physical details of their bodies become almost indistinguishable from those of the surroundings, because the point of view is Dick's and he is thoroughly in touch with the natural world. He even compares Elsie at orgasm to a fish:

> He turned his head so his cheek was flat against her. He could feel her muscles moving softly—her coming was more in her mind still; when she got closer she would become a single band of muscle, like a fish—all of her would move at once, flickering and curving, unified from jaw to tail. . . .
>
> After a while they moved up the bank as though they had to escape the flood. They clambered onto the table of higher ground, onto the spartina. . . . He got his feet out of his pants and made a bed of them for her on the long flattened stalks.

Whether your characters are making it in a salt marsh or between pink satin sheets in a honeymoon hotel in the Poconos, use the physical surroundings the same way a set designer does in a play: to create a mood, to reveal information about who the characters are, and to make the actors moving across the stage as real to us as people in our living room.

3. Your characters don't have to speak to each other but don't forget that they can. The subtitle to this section is *not* Talk Dirty to Me. There is—or should be—a lot more to dialogue between literary lovers than that. Words, Anaïs Nin writes in her diary, "carry colors and sounds into the flesh." When you allow your characters to speak to each other, you can bottle some of that erotic power and add conflict, intrigue, tenderness, humor, just about any mood you want, to your sex scenes. There is nothing like good dialogue to draw us into the world of the book, straight into bed with your characters, which is exactly where you want us to be.

In sex scenes, dialogue can have four important functions:

- It reveals information about who characters are.
- The information it reveals can create conflict between characters or clue us in on the conflict between the lovers and the outside world, as happens in adulterous or other forbidden sex.
- Through dialogue characters can explore and resolve conflicts, or realize they will not be able to resolve them.

- The dialogue can reveal your characters' attitudes toward sex and sexuality, which often affect the course and outcome of a sex scene.

All four are at work in this passage from British writer David Lodge's novel, *Paradise News*, a serious comedy about sexual awakening, religious faith, and the Hawaiian tourist industry. Bernard, a forty-one-year-old virgin and former man of the cloth in Hawaii visiting his dying aunt, gets lessons in love from a vibrant divorcée named Yolande, who is a mental health counselor. They have been meeting for several afternoons in his hotel, and because he is so afraid of sex, she has been introducing him to it slowly, a little each day.

Tomorrow there was more light in the room, and they split a half-bottle of white wine from the minibar before they began. Yolande was bolder and far more loquacious. "Today is still touching only, but nowhere is off-limits, we can touch where we like, how we like, OK? And it needn't be just hands, you can also use your mouth and your tongue. Would you like to suck my breasts? Go ahead. Is that nice? Good, it's nice for me. Can I suck you? Don't worry, I'll squeeze it hard like this and that'll stop you coming. OK. Relax. Was that nice? Good. Sure I like to do it. Sucking and licking are very primal pleasures. Of course, it's easy to see what pleases a man, but with women it's different, it's all hidden inside and you've got to know your way around, so lick your finger, and I'll give you the tour."

He was shocked, bemused, almost physically winded by this sudden acceleration into a tabooless candour of word and gesture. But he was elated too. He hung on for dear life. "Are we going to make love today?" he pleaded.

"This is making love, Bernard," she said. "I'm having a wonderful time, aren't you?"

"Yes, but you know what I mean."

What does dialogue do for this scene?

It's funny and fun to read. It pulls the reader as close to the action as the characters are. It delineates the differences between these two characters and thereby creates just enough gentle conflict to hold our interest and get us involved in the mild struggle between them.

In a reversal of the traditional roles, Yolande is experienced and comfortable—the aggressor. Bernard, overwhelmed by her bluntness and know-how, can only sputter a few words. Their speech reveals who they are and that they are coming to this event with vastly different experience and expectations.

Most cleverly, the dialogue, and particularly Yolande's monologue, make it possible to eliminate clunky sexual stage directions, saving us, the characters and the author the awkward business of "What do you call it?" Had Lodge used a step-by-step format, bits of dialogue followed by stage directions—e.g., "She held his penis in her hand and said, 'Sometimes people suck them,' and bent her head down to his . . ."—the results would have been deadly dull. As it is, we are charmed, amused and maybe a little turned on by forthright Yolande. We probably have some empathy, and maybe a touch of envy, for Bernard, who has no idea what is happening and no idea how much fun he is about to have.

Dialogue should reveal aspects of character, particularly as they relate to how people express, or have difficulty expressing, their sexuality.

The talking that leads up to sex is often more interesting to read about and write about than the thing itself, because there are more possibilities for intrigue and for the unexpected. This is the case in Don DeLillo's *White Noise*, a dark comedy of American "magic and dread," as husband and wife prepare for bed by discussing what erotic literature they will read that night. Their dialogue satirizes both married sex and the "he-entered-her" school of erotic writing. The husband Jack, professor of Hitler studies at a Midwestern university, narrates:

> I said, "Pick your century. Do you want to read about Etruscan slave girls, Georgian rakes? I think we have some literature on flagellation brothels. What about the Middle Ages? We have incubi and succubi. Nuns galore."
>
> "Whatever's best for you."
>
> "I want you to choose. It's sexier that way. . . ."
>
> "I will read," she said. "But I don't want you to choose anything that has men inside women, quote-quote, or men entering women. 'I entered her.' 'He entered me.' We're not lobbies or elevators. 'I wanted him inside me,' as if he could

> crawl completely in, sign the register, sleep, eat, so forth. Can we agree on that? I don't care what these people do as long as they don't enter or get entered."
>
> "Agreed."
>
> " 'I entered her and began to thrust.' "
>
> "I'm in total agreement."
>
> " 'Enter me, enter me, yes, yes.' "
>
> "Silly usage, absolutely."
>
> " 'Insert yourself, Rex. I want you inside me, entering hard, entering deep, yes, now, oh.' "
>
> I began to feel an erection stirring. How stupid and out of context. Babette laughed at her own lines. . . .

In this passage, the dialogue is used to create and resolve a conflict between the characters. Babette insists they read nothing that has "men inside women." Though Jack agrees and says so, the conflict arises when Babette humorously continues to insist, while Jack continues to agree. The result is that Babette gets to say a lot of silly, erotic things that she actually finds objectionable and that ironically have the effect of arousing her husband—the purpose of the erotic readings in the first place. The conflict is resolved in the last paragraph, with Jack aroused and Babette laughing.

Dialogue between lovers need not take place *in bed.* A prelude to a sex scene can tell us more about the nature of your lovers' sexual relationship than a home video.

Dialogue need not be extensive to convey your characters' ardor and attitudes. In this brief passage from Alice Walker's novel, *The Color Purple,* Celie, a poor, uneducated, mistreated young woman, mother and stepmother to many, has her first truly intimate, loving sexual experience with a confident woman named Shug. The novel is in the form of Celie's letters to God, addressing God because she has no one else in whom to confide. Shug has been staying with Celie and her casually brutal husband Albert, who is also Shug's lover. One night when Albert is away, Shug and Celie share a bed and Celie confides the sorrows of her life to Shug, a recitation that ends like this:

> Nobody ever love me, I say.
>
> She say, I love you, Miss Celie. And then she haul off and kiss me on the mouth.

Um, she say, like she surprise. I kiss her back, say, *um*, too.
Us kiss and kiss till us can't hardly kiss no more. Then us
touch each other.

I don't know nothing bout it, I say to Shug.

I don't know much, she say.

Then I feels something real soft and wet on my breast, feel
like one of my little lost babies mouth.

Way after while, I act like a little lost baby too.

Earlier, Celie had told Shug she had hated sex with her husband,
that he never tried to please her—and they never talked about any
of it. The fact that Celie feels safe enough to say anything to Shug
represents a breakthrough for her. The limited dialogue in this passage keeps the focus on the intimacy between the two women and
on their mutual discovery of this new kind of sex. When Celie says to
us, "Then us touch each other" and says to Shug, "I don't know
nothing bout it," we get a vivid sense of the mood of the moment,
Celie's nervousness and anticipation, and the comfort and safety she
feels for the first time in her life.

4. You need not be explicit but you must be specific. "Sex almost
always disappoints me in novels," a well-read psychiatrist told the late
critic Anatole Broyard, in a column in *The New York Times*. "Everything
can be said or done now, and that's what I often find: everything, a
feeling of generality or dispersal. But in my experience, true sex is
so particular, so peculiar to the person who yearns for it. Only he or
she, and no one else, would desire so very much that very person
under those very circumstances. In fiction, I miss that sense of terrific
specificity."

The specific is what makes you fall in love with one person instead
of another. It's what makes walking through Times Square different
from walking through suburban shopping malls with their predictable Banana Republics and Gaps. It's the characteristics that distinguish you from me, and me from the writer who wrote the book you
read before this one.

You create specificity through details, whether they are details that
distinguish one character's dialogue from another or that describe
emotion, action, a landscape, or the feel of mosquitos buzzing
around your main character's recently pierced ear lobe the August

night he loses his virginity in Yellowstone National Park by the light of a full moon.

Though the two are often confused in writing about sex, being specific is different from being explicit. Pornography, in most cases, is an extreme example of the explicit without the specific. It gives us a twitch-by-twitch account of who put what where, with a focus on the welfare and whereabouts of everyone's genitals. It almost never reveals anything that distinguishes one pair of lovers from another, except perhaps in the measurement of sex organs or physical sensations.

This scene by Dorothy Allison is both explicit and specific about larger issues of the character's history and personality as the author stirs sex into her cholesterol-packed celebration of Southern cooking, in a short story, "A Lesbian Appetite." The narrator's wild cravings for dishes flooded with salt, grease and sugar are as powerful as her sexual appetites and often occur simultaneously. The tastes, textures and odors of cooking commingle with those of sex to create a rich sensual stew specific to this character, to her Southern history, and to her exuberant, celebratory nature.

As you read this scene, note that the lines I have underscored suggest the narrator's Southern background and her obsession with fried food.

While the narrator's girlfriend Lee is preparing to cook a too-healthful dish of eggplant and cabbage with safflower oil, the narrator begins using bits of raw eggplant to seduce Lee as she stands at the hot stove.

> We wrestled, eggplant breaking up between our navels. I got her shorts off, she got my jeans down. I dumped a whole plate of eggplant on her belly.
>
> "You are just running salt, girl," I teased, and pushed slices up between her legs, while I licked one of her nipples and pinched the other between a folded slice of eggplant. She was laughing, her belly bouncing under me.
>
> "I'm gonna make you eat all this," she yelled.
>
> "Of course." I pushed eggplant out of the way and slipped two fingers between her labia. She was slicker than peanut oil. "But first we got to get the poison out."
>
> "Oh you!" Her hips rose up into my hand. All her hair had

come loose and was trailing in the flour. She wrapped one hand in my hair, the other around my left breast. "I'll cook you . . . just you wait. I'll cook you a meal to drive you crazy."

"Oh, honey." She tasted like frybread—thick, smoked, and fat-rich on my tongue. . . .

Specificity to time, place, and cultural and geographical circumstances abounds in this sexually explicit scene from *The Mambo Kings Play Songs of Love*, Oscar Hijuelos' melodious novel about a pair of brothers, Cuban immigrants, who become stars of New York's Latino dance halls in the 1950s. From the present day, brother Cesar Castillo is reminiscing about that period, when he and his brother called themselves "the Mambo Kings," in honor of the music they played. Note how Hijuelos incorporates both music and geography (of special interest to immigrants) into this love scene between Castillo and Vanna Vane, a cigarette girl he met in a club. They have just made love, during which "he pumped her so much he tore up the rubber and kept going." A little later the same night:

Smugly, he showed her his *pinga*, as it was indelicately called in his youth. He was sitting on the bed in the Hotel Splendour and leaning back in the shadows, while she was standing by the bathroom door. And just looking at her fine naked body, damp with sweat and happiness, made his big thing all hard again. That thing burning in the light of the window was thick and dark as a tree branch. In those days, it sprouted like a vine from between his legs, carried aloft by a powerful vein that precisely divided his body, and flourished upwards like the spreading top branches of a tree, or, he once thought while looking at a map of the United States, like the course of the Mississippi River and its tributaries.

"Come over here," he told her.

On that night, as on many other nights, he pulled up the tangled sheets so that she could join him on the bed again. And soon Vanna Vane was grinding her damp bottom against his chest, belly, and mouth and strands of her dyed blond hair came slipping down between their lips as they kissed. Then she mounted him and rocked back and forth until things got all twisted and hot inside and both their hearts burst (pounding like conga drums) and they fell back exhausted, resting until they were ready for more, their love-making going around and around in the Mambo King's head, like the melody of a song of love.

How does Hijuelos achieve specificity in this scene?

• He uses an abundance and variety of details to locate Cesar at that youthful, fecund and exciting time of his life. By pointing out twice that all this happened "in those days," he is saying by inference that he is no longer as young, strong or sexually active.

• There is a strong single point of view (Cesar's) through which everything is observed, felt and remembered.

• This celebrated maker of mambo music experiences sex through musical metaphors. Their hearts don't pound like just any drums but like "conga drums." The rhythms of the sentences, particularly the last sentence, are lush and exuberant and suggest an openness to sensation and emotion that is also characteristic of mambo music.

• Cesar's status as a recent arrival is reinforced by his comparing the vein of his penis to a tributary of the Mississippi River. While anyone might reasonably study a map, a newcomer is likely to look at it with fresh eyes and a greater sense of wonder than someone more familiar with the country.

• The detail of Vanna Vane's dyed blonde hair, mentioned in this passage only in passing, becomes an important characteristic several paragraphs later. Cesar remembers that in those days "to be seen with a woman like Vanna was prestigious as a passport, a high-school diploma, a full-time job, a record contract, a 1951 DeSoto." Immigrants hungry for this kind of prestige will take—or will have to settle for—a dyed blonde, not the real thing. Just as Cesar knows he is not a "Real American," Vanna is not a Real Blonde.

In a much less sexually explicit scene in a short story by Ethan Canin, "We are Nighttime Travelers," an elderly husband and wife estranged for many years—"There have been three Presidents since I held her in my arms"—rediscover one another. The husband narrates.

I do not say anything. Instead I roll in the bed, reach across, and touch her, and because she is surprised she turns to me.

> When I kiss her the lips are dry, cracking against mine, unfamiliar as the ocean floor. But then the lips give. They part. I am inside her mouth, and there, still hidden from the world, as if ruin had forgotten a part, it is wet—Lord! I have the feeling of a miracle. Her tongue comes forward. I do not know myself then, what man I am, who I lie with in embrace. I can barely remember her beauty. She touches my chest and I bite lightly on her lip, spread moisture to her cheek and then kiss there. She makes something like a sigh. "Frank," she says. "Frank." We are lost now in seas and deserts. My hand finds her fingers and grips them, bone and tendon, fragile things.

Without knowing much more about these characters, this brief, complete and very specific description, exclusively from the husband's point of view, tells us a great deal about who they are: elderly, fragile, once intimate, and more excited and tenderly disposed than either might have expected. The husband's feelings of expansiveness at this moment are conveyed in part through metaphors about the ocean floor, seas and deserts, places so vast and elemental that they suggest immeasurable depth and history, which could parallel the history of a marriage. Particularly moving is the wife's eagerness and the husband's joyous but silent surprise as he encounters it.

Whether your lovers are young and randy or old and infirm, their familiar journey toward sexual connection should be anything but predictable, in large measure because you create it using details and a voice that are specific to *these* characters at *this* particular moment in their lives and in the story.

5. Surprise me. In real life, we generally enjoy the company of congenial people, but when we read literature, we often prefer characters who are difficult, vexing, selfish, self-involved, diabolical, ambitious, vain—complex creations who cause themselves and those around them trouble. The trouble can be as vast and destructive as Captain Ahab's obsession with the whale in Herman Melville's *Moby Dick*, or as quietly irksome as Bartleby's refusal to say anything other than, "I would prefer not to," in Melville's short story, "Bartleby the Scrivener."

But whether our characters' demons are internal or external, whether they are extraordinary people or ordinary people faced with extraordinary challenges, we are drawn to the conflict that swirls around them. On an emotional level, it engages our curiosity and possibly our sympathy, if not for the most difficult characters then for their victims. On a technical level, the conflict created by these characters helps move the story forward. What will he do next? we wonder. How will he get out of *this* one? we ask ourselves and keep turning the pages. The most compelling characters in fiction are often their own worst enemies: They antagonize, alienate, throw metaphorical bricks through metaphorical windows. Or real snowballs that set in motion a series of accidents, births and deaths that occupy Robertson Davies' characters throughout his best-known long work, *The Deptford Trilogy.*

But whether their gestures are large or small, the best characters continually surprise us, even if it is only with their own stubbornness. And they continually create conflict for themselves and everyone in their midst.

When you lead your characters into bed together, these same dynamics must happen in miniature. When writing about these few intimate moments, which are not generally characterized by conflict, you must nevertheless create some kind of conflict, tension or surprise, whether it is in the language, the relationship between the characters, the relationship between a pair of lovers and the hostile outside world, or between a narrator and the lovers whose story you are telling, as happens in James Salter's highly erotic novel, *A Sport and a Pastime,* discussed in chapter eight.

There are no surprises in pornography: Everything moves inexorably toward the orgasm. A well-written sex scene in a more literary book or story manages to rewrite pornography's punchline so that we remember not the force of the characters' orgasms but the thing that happened that we didn't expect, what I'm calling The Surprise. The Surprise, though, is not a single, discrete entity. Good writing offers all kinds of surprises and pleasures—of scene, plot, character and language—and good writing about sex does too.

Most readers, I imagine, were startled by this very brief scene about halfway into the popular Danish thriller by Peter Hoeg, *Smilla's Sense of Snow,* which Smilla, a female sleuth, narrates:

> Standing in the middle of the bedroom, we take off each other's clothes.

He has a light, fumbling brutality, which several times makes me think that this time it'll cost me my sanity. In our dawning, mutual intimacy, I induce him to open the little slit in the head of his penis so I can put my clitoris inside and fuck him.

With that eerie multiple role reversal (the author is a man), the chapter ends. The unusual physical connection is indeed a surprise to us, but it is not a gratuitous surprise because it fits with Smilla's character: She has renounced the traditional passive female role, whether she's investigating a crime or falling in love.

Moving to a much larger canvas, one of the most erotically charged sexual encounters in all of literature, in *Madame Bovary*, has its own unique surprise: In it we see nothing at all of the impassioned lovers, only the horse-drawn carriage that thunders through the streets of nineteenth-century Rouen, rocked and rolled, propelled by the force of the lovemaking unleashed inside it.

Let's look at some of the more ordinary surprises good writers spring on us, often so subtly we aren't aware of it, in order to give depth and texture to their sex scenes. This list covers broad categories, and clearly some examples are appropriate for more than one category. In your own reading and writing, you will certainly encounter other kinds of surprises.

• **The Surprise of Action.** In which something occurs that shifts our attention away from the orgasm or from the mechanics of sex. The action or occurrence might be as dramatic as a cuckolded husband leaping out of a bedroom closet at the moment of truth or as inert as a wife falling asleep while her husband makes love to her, as in John Updike's *Rabbit is Rich*.

• **The Surprise of Speech.** In which characters speak while making love, which again can shift the focus away from the predictable mechanics of sex. As with all good dialogue, dialogue in this setting should be there for a reason integral to the characters and the story. We should learn something about the characters or their circumstances from what they say to one another in bed. In Scott Turow's *Presumed Innocent*, narrator Rusty Sabitch remembers his torrid, illicit affair with Carolyn Polhemus, whose murder he is accused of committing. In recounting their sex life, he tells us that she used to "roam, take my penis in her mouth, let it go, and slide her hand past my scrotum, probing in that hole." Then she would cruelly ask, "Does Barbara [his wife] do this for you?" Rusty understood her comment to be a manipulative and disarming play in their power struggle, leaving Rusty humiliated and exposed. Carolyn, he tells us, "could bring my wife into our bed and make her one more witness to how much I was willing to abandon." Later, when Carolyn invites Rusty to make love to her anally, she repeats the line, "Does Barbara do this for you?" which reveals her skill at manipulating and controlling him by exploiting the shame he feels for betraying his wife.

• **The Surprise of Distraction.** A character becomes distracted by something or someone. The noise of a child upstairs; a lover's tears; a memory; a nearby object; a disturbing thought.

• **The Surprise of Insight.** In which a description of a sexual encounter includes an insight or important observation, as when Rusty Sabitch admits that "after seventeen years of faithful marriage, of wandering impulse suppressed for the sake of tranquil domestic life, I could not believe that I was here, with fantasy made real . . . in the land beyond restraint, rescued from the diligent, slowly moving circles of my life. Each time I entered [Carolyn], I felt I divided the world."

• **The Surprise of Language.** Because we create with language, not oil paint and not stone, the necessary surprise need not involve an unexpected turn of events, but only an unexpected turn of phrase. Our goal should not be cleverness or verbal contrivance but original language and metaphor that demand our attention, words that are particularly eloquent in doing what our words are meant to do: move the reader to feel what the character feels at that moment, whether it is arousal, excitement, melancholy, fear or revulsion. The surprise of language at its most eloquent, inventive and/or metaphorical forces the reader to think about sex in a way she has not before, as when novelist James Salter, in *A Sport and a Pastime,* says of the lovers Dean and Anne-Marie: "He kisses her side and then, without force, as one stirs a favorite mare, begins again. She comes to life with a soft, exhausted sound, like someone saved from drowning." Later in the novel, as they make love, "She begins to roll her hips, to cry out. It's like ministering to a lunatic."

In this description from *Written on the Body* by British novelist Jeanette Winterson, we are very conscious of the presence of the writer—the creator of these many metaphors—but far from distancing the reader, the vividness and aptness of the metaphors and the active involvement of the "I" lure us into the narrator's rich sexual and sensory life. Note the enlarging movement in the metaphors from animals (cats and horses) to sea life and finally to the tides, which suggest sensual, undulating movement and the predictable, repetitive cycles we find both in lust and in nature.

> She arches her body like a cat on a stretch. She nuzzles her cunt into my face like a filly at the gate. She smells of the sea. She smells of rockpools when I was a child. She keeps a starfish in there. I crouch down to taste the salt, to run my fingers around the rim. She opens and shuts like a sea anemone. She's refilled each day with fresh tides of longing.

In a very different example, the language is so stark and stripped down it comes close to dispensing with the illusion that we are reading an account. In this scene from "Home," an early short story by Jayne Anne Phillips, I feel so close to the narrator and the dream she relates that I flinch every time I read it. She is a recent college graduate living reluctantly with her aging, divorced mother. Though the young woman has had lovers, she has never had an orgasm. She remembers having a dream:

> My father comes to me in a dream. He kneels beside me, touches my mouth. He turns my face gently toward him.
> Let me see, he says. Let me see it.
> He is looking for a scar, a sign. He wears only a towel around his waist. He presses himself against my thigh, pretending solicitude. But I know what he is doing; I turn my head in repulsion and stiffen. He smells of sour musk and his forearms are black with hair. I think to myself, It's been years since he's had an erection—
> Finally he stands. Cover yourself, I tell him.
> I can't, he says, I'm hard.

The scene ends there, with a patch of white space, the words "I'm hard" hanging ominously in the air, leaving us as disturbed as the narrator is by this dream. Though she never tells us whether the dream re-enacts scenes of genuine abuse, we sense a sexual disturbance in the household, a hint as to the cause of her failure to have satisfying sexual relationships. The language of the scene is so straightforward it feels more like we are experiencing this event—dreaming this dream—ourselves.

What is interesting emotionally about this dream is that it is not the simple account of aggressor and victim. Most compelling is not the father's approach to the girl or her turning him away, but what happens *after* she turns him away. Far from expressing distaste for what has happened, although we know she feels it, she becomes more of an adult participant, less of a victim, when she thinks: "It's been years since he's had an erection." Rather than telling him to get out of her room or out of her life—a wholesale rejection— she equivocates: "Cover yourself," as if to say, "I want you to stay but I don't want to see more evidence of your desire right now." By not rejecting him outright, she is, in some sense, acknowledging her own desire and arousal. This may be as disturbing to her and to us as the father's violation.

• **Combination Surprise Platter.** Philip Roth's succés de scandale, *Portnoy's Complaint,* includes a scene that touches on every possible kind of surprise known to young men *and* writers. Teenage Alex Portnoy, who is totally obsessed with masturbation, goes with a group of friends to visit a prostitute, having been told by the boy who arranged the trip that they will all "get laid."

Far from losing his virginity in this scene, young Portnoy ends up with a tired hooker named Bubbles who is ready to go home. She refuses to do anything but masturbate him. Once she begins and sees it might take a while—"it is like trying to jerk off a jelly-fish," he confesses—she ups the stakes and says he has only fifty seconds in which to finish. The only way he can manage to arouse himself is by fantasizing about masturbating. But when he is finally at the point of orgasm, she says, " 'Okay, that's it . . . fifty,' *and stops!*" He begs for another few seconds. " 'Look, I already ironed two hours, you know, before you guys even got here—' " She will not give in. "Whereupon, unable (as always!) to stand the frustra-tion—the deprivation and disappointment—I reach down, I grab it, and POW!" Not only is he reduced to doing it himself—"I ask you, who jerks me off as well as I do it myself?"—but he suffers another indignity when "the jet . . . lands with a thick wet burning splash right in my own eye." Almost every line of this scene serves up something unexpected, and the stakes keep rising higher and higher. " 'Son of a bitch kike,' Bubbles screams. 'You got gissum all over the couch! And the walls! And the lamp!' " Portnoy is not only worried about the possibility of going blind—but about the personal and historical implications of being called a kike. And on and on it goes. Roth manages to turn the cliché of the teenage boy's first visit to a whore into a rich, sidesplittingly funny scene that leads us back again to the themes of the novel, the struggle between being a good Jew and a good Jewish son and being as naughty as your libido begs you to be.

The arrival of AIDS into our lives has forced a sea change in sexual behavior and attitudes and has had a profound effect on what many of us write when we write about sex these days. In the next chapter, we will take a look at some of the literary challenges AIDS creates for us.

CHAPTER FOUR

The End of Bravado

Writing About Sex in the Age of AIDS

". . . he never mentioned the prospect that even if he didn't die . . . that whatever happened it was over, the way he had lived until now . . . the end of bravado, the end of folly, the end of trusting life. . . ."
—Susan Sontag, "The Way We Live Now"

A fiction editor at a national magazine reports with some dismay that she is seeing an abundance of short story submissions in which plots turn on couples, exclusively heterosexual, deciding not to have sex because they don't have a condom and ending their evenings together with harsh words and recriminations over the matter. The rubber used as an artifice to end a date rings false to the editor; so do all the women characters who cross her desk who do not carry their own condoms, as many do in real life. By contrast, the editor notes that in stories about gay men, the absence of a condom is not enough to ruffle anyone's feathers or cut short a date. In a community decimated by AIDS, safe sex is de rigueur, and creative solutions to lust essential.

What does all this mean when it comes to devising a few general principles on writing about sex in the age of AIDS? To begin with, it means that how you and your characters approach sex *and* safe sex depends very much on your relationship to the disease. Gay characters, and the largely gay writers who create them, live in an environment in many ways defined by the ravages and repercussions of AIDS.

Illness and death have an inescapable immediacy and weight for the infected and uninfected alike; fictional characters, like their real-life counterparts, often exist in extremis, forced to explore the fusion of love, sex, mortality and grief.

To most of the straight characters in fiction published up to now, when it is mentioned at all, AIDS has been a much more distant threat, something that doesn't much come to their minds except when they are contemplating sex with a new partner. The act of practicing safe sex—or quarreling over practicing it—is often the most tangible connection to the disease these characters have.

The AIDS-aware fiction I have read led me to organize this chapter around the differences between these two communities as they have emerged to date in fiction. Of course these characteristics and the fiction that explores them may well change in years to come.

A minute subgroup of fictional characters to emerge so far are heterosexual adults infected with HIV or AIDS. Though AIDS-infected children have made appearances (in Alice Hoffman's novel, *At Risk*, and a recent first novel, *Rocking the Babies*, by Linda Raymond), my research turned up only one short story, "Pandora's Box," by Janice Eidus (in the 1994 *O. Henry Prize Short Story Collection*) and one novel, *Touch*, by Charlotte Watson Sherman, published by HarperCollins in 1995, with heterosexual, HIV-positive adults, in both cases women, one of whom is sexually active.

Before examining the demands of writing about sex and safe sex in both categories, it's important to note that because we can track the emergence of AIDS and our awareness of it so precisely, the year in which you set a work of fiction is crucial to whether and how the issue of AIDS will be incorporated into your characters' behavior and attitudes. The cutoff dates will vary between gays and straights, and break down even further by the country or even city in which you set a work of fiction. Alan Hollinghurst tells us in *The Swimming Pool Library* that his narrator is writing about the summer of 1983 in England, "the last summer of its kind there was ever to be." AIDS is never mentioned, but our certain knowledge of what is to come in-fuses his sex scenes with the possibility of extinction and with an added poignancy. Like today's readers of Christopher Isherwood's *Berlin Stories*, based on his experiences living in Berlin from 1929 to

1933 and published in 1939, we know something about what is to come that the characters, and in Isherwood's case the author, do not.

THE GAY COMMUNITY

AIDS has been chronicled so powerfully in fiction by writers from Reynolds Price and Edmund White to Allen Barnett and Christopher Coe (two of many gifted young writers who have died of AIDS), that I come to the task of giving any writerly advice on the subject tugging my forelock. My hunch is that gay writers need less guidance than others in certain aspects of writing about sex these days because they possess an abundance of charged material: an enforced code of sexual behavior in which desire and grief have become permanently linked. Under these circumstances, it is not difficult to apply the principle of making a sex scene matter to your characters and the larger concerns of your story. It matters unrelentingly. For the protagonist in Edmund White's story "Running on Empty," "These days, of course, desire entailed hopelessness—he'd learned to match every pant of longing with a sigh of regret."

As you study the examples below from recent fiction, consider the following observations and guidelines in addition to the basic principles of good writing about sex described in chapters two and three, *which apply here as well*:

1. Practicing safe sex seems to be taken for granted among gay male characters. Little conflict erupts between them around this issue except in the case of the occasional daredevil who wants to have unprotected sex. Because the norm of safe sex has been so firmly established, when a character rejects it, we should have some idea what is motivating him. Occasionally, notably in a story called "Succor" by Allen Barnett, characters negotiate beforehand what constitutes safe sex.

2. As in all sex scenes, if you go into the physical details, whether or not they refer specifically to elements of safe sex, the details should enhance the story in some way: by helping create dramatic tension and/or revealing something about the relationship, the culture and the characters.

3. As in all good fiction involving sex, if you create the world beyond the bedroom with sufficient depth and texture, you will have

more to work with when your characters seek each other out behind closed doors. This is particularly true in a setting as freighted and overdetermined as this one.

4. In quite a bit of gay fiction, sex scenes include explicit references to illness or death, but it is certainly not necessary to be explicit to convey the ways in which they bear down upon your characters' sexual selves.

As I look over the following excerpts from two recent short stories, I see that what unites them is a meticulous degree of attention to character. Each character's role in the scene flows from everything about him that has come before, creating a sense of inevitability that distinguishes the best fiction.

Grief, lust, sexual terror, and a self-mocking search for innocence are at the heart of Wesley Gibson's whimsically devastating story "Out There." Billy, the guarded, ironic protagonist who makes decorative furniture designed *not* to last, has watched his attitudes change in recent years from "cheerful pessimism to this, whatever it was," because of his proximity to so much death. After breaking up with his latest lover, in a pancake house, he now wants to "date," by which he means, as he explains to his friend Clare, "real dates with going to the movies and kisses goodnight and no sex." He describes a date with a man he calls John Day:

> They didn't make it to the movies. Billy tried: "I don't think we should sleep together on the first date," feeling like Linda Lovelace disguised as Sandra Dee. John Day was not put off by Billy's disguise. He'd said, "Why not?" smiling and pulling Billy gently towards him by the collar. John Day had a sly, giddy smile that had disarmed Sandra Dees from time immemorial. He kissed warm and tough. He'd tested negative. It was good-bye Troy Donahue and volleyball on the beach. It was hello Deep Throat. It was hello darkness.
> They kept losing their erections.

The sense of growing sexual abandon that the author creates in the long paragraph, with Billy resisting at first and then tumbling to John's advances, is a nice setup for the punchline, which is that they are both too frightened to go through with it, even *with* safe sex. Sex used to be a fleeting respite for lovers to forget their troubles for a short while, but for gay men in these times, it has become instead a chilling reminder of loss and potential loss.

When Billy and John meet again, "They also couldn't come. After an hour or so, they subsided into caresses, Billy rubbing little circles on John Day's belly, John Day kneading the back of Billy's neck." In the meantime, Billy has also begun dating another John ("John Two") who, he learns in short order, has tested positive. When John asks him, " 'Does it matter?' " and Billy answers no, "He could have been lying. He didn't know." It leads Billy to these thoughts:

> Love. Even as a joke, it kicked up a dust of confusion. There was a time when Billy could have said, "This is love. This is grief. Here's one of me having fun." But now all his loves were streaked with grief; and all his griefs shot through with a terrible love. This borderless place he'd been shoved into was identical to the place before, but the old maps were useless, the language was subtly different; and he stumbled over the future tense of its verbs.

In this startling passage from "The *Times* as It Knows Us," by Allen Barnett, about a group of gay friends recently portrayed—inaccurately, they feel—in *The New York Times*, the narrator recalls his beloved lover Samuel, who died of AIDS, and wonders how he and others can mourn their multitudinous losses. "Our condolences are arid as leaves," he thinks. "We are actors who have over-rehearsed our lines." He remembers a friend urging him not to attend the funeral of a man he did not know well; but he knew it would have been perilous to deny his own grief. To survive, he realizes he must:

> Give sorrow occasion and let it go, or your heart will imprison you in constant February, a chain-link fence around frozen soil, where your dead will stack in towers past the point of grieving. *Let your tears fall for the dead, and as one who is suffering begin the lament . . . do not neglect his burial.* Think of him, the one you loved, on his knees, on his elbows, his face turned up to look back in yours, his mouth dark in his dark beard. He was smiling because of you. You tied a silky rope around his wrists, then down around the base of his cock and balls, his anus raised for you. When you put your mouth against it, you ceased to exist. All else fell away. You had

brought him, and he you, to that point where you are most your mind and most your body. His prostate pulsed against your fingers like a heart in a cave, *mind, body, body, mind,* over and over. Looking down at him, he who is dead and gone, then lying across the broken bridge of his spine, the beach-head of his back, you would gladly change places with him. *Let your weeping be bitter and your wailing fervent; then be comforted for your sorrow.* Find in grief the abandon you used to find in love; grieve the way you used to fuck.

In the way that AIDS has forced many to reinvent sexuality, this passage presents the possibility for a new literary form to accommodate the horror of AIDS: a sex scene that is part elegy and part prayer for the dead, and that concludes with some raw, practical, self-help style advice on learning to live with grief.

THE STRAIGHT WORLD

In my conversations with writers about this chapter, many heterosexuals among them have said they are stumped about how to handle safe sex in their work, safe sex being the only brush with the threat of AIDS in most of their characters' lives. What I think they want to know is how to overcome the awkwardness, inelegance and unspontaneousness of safe sex and not call so much attention to the condom, the logistics, and the seriousness of the threat that everyone involved ceases to have a good time.

Though in real life some teenagers and adults practice safe sex with new partners, it is not the essential gesture it is in the gay community. Thus it seems, in real life and in fiction, every encounter with a new partner is a potential wrangle over who requires safe sex, who doesn't, and exactly what it is. In Charlotte Watson Sherman's novel, *Touch,* her protagonist, Rayna, an African-American painter in her thirties, has what she calls "The Talk" with each new lover: She says she won't make love unless he wears a condom. When a recent suitor "failed" the talk—refused to wear one—Rayna walked away. But with her new man, perhaps smarting from her last rejection, "she couldn't bring herself to say the words." They don't spring to his lips either.

This issue, of learning to write about AIDS and the threat of AIDS in a largely uninfected community, is very much a work in progress.

For the time being, I offer these guidelines as a place to begin:

1. If you are not on the sexual front lines these days, do some research: Talk to people who are. Ask them what takes place in their intimate exchanges around this issue. Obviously, there is no one scenario, but getting a sense of the atmosphere and possibilities may help you create the right scenario for your characters, in keeping with who they are.

2. Whether or not you do research, explore your own reactions to this issue and *use those feelings* in developing your characters' actions and reactions. If, for example, you feel awkward, self-conscious, and preoccupied with regret that sex has come to this—remember: Your characters might feel that way too.

3. Don't be politically correct and artistically feeble. It's not enough for your characters to carry condoms and take them out at the appropriate moment. Use the device and the issue to enrich the work, to bring us closer to the characters and the moment.

4. If you are writing about characters who are infected, feelings of fear, illness and loss may be more immediate.

5. If writing about safe sex seems as confining as having it may, surprise us—and yourself—and have some fun with it, as Australian writer Peter Carey does in this passage from his novel, *The Tax Inspector.*

Toward the end of the novel, a very unlikely union has developed between Maria Takis and Jack Catchprice. She's a left-leaning tax inspector, eight months pregnant and no longer seeing the married man who fathered her child. Jack, a slick, successful, real estate developer, is kin to (though not in business with) the crazy, eccentric Catchprice family, who own a failing car dealership whose illegal accounting methods have come to the attention of the tax inspector. In Jack's bed late at night, Maria is self-conscious about her body and reluctant to sleep with someone whose values are so alien to her own. She professes to be too pregnant to concentrate on his seduction. He answers:

> "We could try. We could just lie here."
> "I don't know you. . . . It's not smart for people to just jump into bed any more."

"Is this a discussion about the Unmentionable?"

"I don't want to offend you."

"You don't offend me at all. We could play it safe."

"Saf*er*, not actually safe," she smiled. While still involved in her monogamous adulterous relationship with Alistair, she had complacently pitied those who must go through this. She had never thought that the tone of the conversation might be quite so tender.

He touched her on the forehead between her eyes and ran his finger down the line of her nose. "I'll make love to you 100 per cent safe."

She had never imagined you could say those words and still feel tender, but now she was lying on her side and he was lying on his and he had those clear blue Catchprice eyes and such sweet crease marks around his eyes. . . .

"Is there 100 per cent?" she asked.

"Is this safe?"

"Mmm?"

"Does this feel safe?"

"Jack, don't."

"Don't worry. I'll keep my word. Is this safe?"

"Of course."

She let him undress her and caress her swollen body. God, she thought—this is how people die.

"Is this beautiful to you?"

"Oh yes," he said. "You glisten. . . ."

. . . She began to kiss him, to kiss his chest, to nuzzle her face among the soft apple-sweet hairs, discovering as she did so a hunger for the scents and textures of male skin.

"Get the condom," she heard herself say.

"You sure?"

"Mmm."

"I've got it."

"I'm crazy," she said.

The passage, one of the few extended fictional exchanges involving heterosexual safe sex, and by far the most interesting, uses Maria's embarrassment, awkwardness and fear to create the dramatic conflict that drives the scene. The exchange is full of surprises. My favorite is

Maria's final "yes," which manages to rewrite for the age of AIDS Molly Bloom's great announcement of openness to sexual passion in James Joyce's *Ulysses*—"yes I said yes I will yes"—to this: "Get the condom."

The abundance of dialogue creates an intimacy and immediacy that draws us right into bed with Maria and Jack. They surprise one another and the reader with their mix of nervousness (Maria's), suaveness (Jack's), collective good humor and tenderness. Safe sex is both serious and playful in a way that accurately reflects the degree of danger these characters feel.

How fiction writers of the future will incorporate HIV and AIDS into their characters' sex lives will depend very much on what course the disease takes in real life. For the time being, recent literature suggests that those venturing into this territory have a few more choices than they might have imagined.

The remainder of this book will concentrate on techniques for writing about sex, and strategies for reading, that focus on the relationship between sexual partners. I begin each chapter with a discussion of what characterizes the relationship and what these characteristics mean to a fiction writer—what possibilities they offer us. Next, I list some "Given Circumstances," what I think of as general truths about such a relationship we need to incorporate into our sex scenes. Not every given circumstance will be true in every case, but many will be. Following the list are examples of writing meant to illustrate particular points and give you a range of the possibilities for combining the general with the specific.

While I separate the issue of writing about sex in the age of AIDS from the chapters to come on types of relationships, I mean for the guidelines I offer here to supplement those that follow.

CHAPTER FIVE

Losing Your Cherry

First Times to Remember

"Leota was bold. She wasn't afraid to touch anything and where her knowledge came from was a secret but she knew what she was after. And I soon found out."

—Rita Mae Brown, *Rubyfruit Jungle*

Losing one's virginity has more in common with getting a driver's license than we like to think. The plastic-sealed card that fits in your wallet doesn't mean you know all you need to know about driving; it means you've been given permission to find out firsthand everything you don't know.

First-time lovers, even if they are married, are usually young, nervous, and doing the deed in either unfamiliar or uncomfortable surroundings: the bridal suite, the back seat of a car, the teenager's narrow twin bed or the prostitute's chamber. Put another way, no one's first time is likely to be a sexual tsunami. It's not supposed to be; it's just supposed to push you through the starting gate and get you going. It may be over not long after it begins. For women it may be extremely painful. Or it may be so unsatisfactory that it leaves one or both partners scratching their heads and wondering if they misread the directions, as a pair of newlyweds does in Joseph Heller's satiric novel about World War II, *Catch 22*, until Doc Daneeka shows them, with the aid of rubber models in his office, what goes where.

What does all this mean for the fiction writer? It means you don't have to worry about writing a sex scene so hot you'd be embarrassed to show it to your mother. It means there are some interesting possibilities for conflict and drama between the lovers involving one's experience versus the other's innocence; one's timidity against the other's temerity; her nonchalance bumping up against his fear. It means your characters are very likely to be in a heightened state of awareness—accentuating feelings of awkwardness and self-consciousness—because, after all, this is a once-in-a-lifetime thing. This is a Big Deal. This is the jackknife off the high diving board. But, of course, it's almost always a disappointment, until you get the hang of it.

Because first times are so much about these new physical sensations, your fictional characters are likely to be paying a lot of attention to their genitals, not because they are powerhouses of pleasure but because we know they are supposed to be, and we want to be sure to be paying attention in case the transformation happens. It's like a child in a car asking "Are we there yet?" During your first time, particularly if you're female, you're not sure if you're there yet.

We only ever get one First Time, but there can be more than one *kind* of first time: the technical initiation versus what I call "The First Time That Matters" or "The First Time I Understood Why This Was Such A Big Deal," which may occur years later. In this section I've included a second chance at first times from a short story by Edmund White.

For young people learning about sex and love in America these days, it is difficult to convey how much a woman's—though not a man's—virginity used to mean, and how many classic works of fiction, from Samuel Richardson's eighteenth-century epistolary novel *Clarissa*, to Thomas Hardy's nineteenth-century *Tess of the D'Urbervilles* (subtitled, *A Pure Woman*), turn on the loss or threatened loss of female virtue, synonymous back then with virginity. "The debauching of a virgin may be her ruin and make her for life unhappy," said Benjamin Franklin in his essay, "Advice on the Choice of a Mistress." The injustice of the double standard was not lost on early twentieth-century anarchist and socialist Emma Goldman in her essay "The Traffic in Women":

> Society considers the sex experiences of a man as attri-
> butes of his general development, while similar experiences

in the life of a woman are looked upon as a terrible calamity, a loss of honor and of all that is good and noble in a human being.

In her celebrated novel *The Group*, Mary McCarthy, who wrote scorchingly about women's sex lives long before birth control pills were a gleam in anyone's eye, presented a group of Vassar graduates in the 1930s. Their ideas about sex were shaped by both the boldness of the roaring twenties and the ignorance of the Victorian era, when British wives were advised to "grip the bed and think of England" to endure their marital duties. In a scene from *The Group* too long to be included here, Dottie Renfrew, known as "Boston," class of '33, is eager to lose her virginity to the best man at her classmate's wedding, Dick Brown, who, she thinks, "was so frightfully attractive and unhappy and had so much to give."

When I was twelve years old, this scene was passed around as the smut of our day, and particularly the passage after which Dick deflowers Dottie, examines the sheet beneath her and says, referring to another girlfriend, this one quite unlucky, "Betty bled like a pig." I knew that sex had occurred but knew nothing of hymens and their properties and read this line at least six hundred times, my brow permanently wrinkled in bemusement. When I read the scene again last summer, Betty bleeding like a pig was of no consequence compared to the wicked dialogue and McCarthy's wry feminist leanings. Dottie is so naïve she has no idea how badly Dick is treating her and no idea she has had an orgasm until he tells her. Even then she is not convinced:

> "You *came*, Boston," he remarked. . . . "I mean you had an orgasm." Dottie made a vague, still-inquiring noise in her throat; she was pretty sure, now, she understood, but the new word discombobulated her. "A climax," he added, more sharply. "Do they teach you that word at Vassar?. . ." "It's normal then?" she wanted to know, beginning to feel better. Dick shrugged. "Not for girls of your upbringing. Not the first time, usually. Appearances to the contrary, you're probably highly sexed."

Reading this scene again, all I could think was, "Dirty books are wasted on the young."

GIVEN CIRCUMSTANCES

1. Particularly when it's a woman's first time with a man, it's almost certain sex will *not* be the sizzling, earth-moving variety. For the woman it may feel more like a surgical procedure without anesthesia.
2. The first time is a major rite of passage. People often have great expectations for it and devote a good bit of time afterwards wondering if the actuality met their expectations—the Before-and-After exercise. Because of these expectations, people are in a heightened state of awareness.
3. It's likely the characters don't know each other well.
4. One or both may be young, timid, anxious, ignorant, and/or fearful, afraid of the unknown, of pregnancy, disease or being caught.
5. The setting isn't often a place of one's own.
6. Customs and expectations about the first time vary with age, gender, religion and cultural background.
7. For gays and lesbians and others for whom sex is forbidden, the first time may have complex elements of anxiety, guilt, shame, rebellion, relief and/or liberation.

EXAMPLES

Though not especially graphic, there is no ambiguity about what happens in this scene from Sandra Cisneros' story "One Holy Night," from her collection, *Woman Hollering Creek*. A Mexican-American girl about thirteen is recounting her first time, legally an instance of statutory rape, for which she paid with pregnancy and banishment to Mexico, where she waits now for her baby to be born. In Chicago, she had worked her family's cucumber and mango pushcart and fallen for a young Mexican national who professed to be in love with the mythology and history of his people. He called himself Chaq Uxmal Paloquin and claimed he was from "an ancient line of Mayan kings."

Here's what happens to our naïve, plucky and nameless narrator in Chaq's rented room behind Esparza & Son Auto Repair:

> You must not tell anyone what I am going to do, he said.
> And what I remember next is how the moon, the pale moon with its one yellow eye, the moon of Tikal, and Tulum, and

Chichén, stared through the pink plastic curtains. Then
something inside bit me, and I gave out a cry as if the other,
the one I wouldn't be anymore, leapt out.

So I was initiated beneath an ancient sky by a great and
mighty heir—Chaq Uxmal Paloquin. I, Ixchel, his queen.

The section ends here and after a white space, picks up in a very
different tone, one completely lacking in romance and illusion:

The truth is, it wasn't a big deal. It wasn't any deal at all. I
put my bloody panties inside my T-shirt and ran home hug-
ging myself. I thought about a lot of things on the way home.
I thought about all the world and how suddenly I became a
part of history. . . .

. . . I know I was supposed to feel ashamed, but I wasn't
ashamed. I wanted to stand on top of the highest building,
the top-top floor, and yell, *I know.*

Then I understood why Abuelita didn't let me sleep over
at Lourdes's house full of too many brothers, and why the
Roman girl in the movies always runs away from the soldier,
and what happens when the scenes in love stories begin to
fade, and why brides blush, and how it is that sex isn't simply
a box you check *M* or *F* on in the test we get at school.

The girl, who is in the eighth grade, has left her mango pushcart
at Chaq's place; when she returns to her grandmother's house
without it, it becomes the evidence and symbol of her downfall.

In this scene, as in most moving accounts of first times, the physical
details of body meeting body are less important than the character's
evolving psychological state. The challenge for you the writer is to
capture the arc of anticipation, heightened awareness and, perhaps,
disappointment, without resorting to clichés.

Look over the list of given circumstances. How many apply to this
scene?

1. Penetration is painful.
2. The character plays a delightful version of the Before-and-After
   game. The earth has not moved and Chaq is no angel, but her
   perceptions are altered forever. Her grandmother's annoying
   rules suddenly make sense; the behavior of characters in

      movies is motivated now by nature, not whimsy. She grows up
      in a matter of minutes.

3. The characters do not know each other well. She soon learns
    his very unglamorous name is Chato, which means "fat-face,"
    he has no Mayan blood, he is thirty-seven and a dangerous
    criminal.

4. She also does not realize that her first time is actually statutory
    rape and that his demand that she not tell anyone is coercive.
    Though she is not fearful of the act or its consequences at the
    time, before long they catch up with her. Because she is still a
    child, she has to fear her grandmother's authority when she
    comes home without the pushcart, and without her virginity.

5. The unfamiliar setting sharpens her senses, heightens her
    awareness of the event.

6. Her Mexican-American and Catholic upbringing have
    groomed her to be "ashamed" of what she has done. She
    rejects that.

If a good sex scene must surprise us, what kind of surprises do we
find here? First, Cisneros rewrites the clichés. She pays homage to
the clichés of a girl's first time, but puts her own unique twist on
them. The girl notices the moon but Cisneros makes sure it is not
just any moon. It's the moon of the Mayan civilizations Chaq professes
to descend from and that the girl, in her youthful naiveté, believes
are his. Cisneros might have allowed the girl's romanticization of
Chaq to dominate the moment; instead she yanks us back into the
grim reality of the present by juxtaposing the exotic moon to the
pink plastic curtains of the rented room.

    Next, Cisneros lets the girl reject the conventions of her up-
bringing. Had Cisneros made her wallow in the shame and guilt she
was programmed to feel, she would have limited her emotional reg-
ister. By refusing to give the girl that predictable, narrow range of
self-reproachful feelings, Cisneros not only asserts that she is different
but then allows her feelings and observations to wander and multiply,
to expand in richness and originality.

    We can take two lessons from this example. First, beware the clichés
of first-time love. Avoid them completely or, as Cisneros does, give
them a unique twist. Second, when you allow your characters to reject
the sexual mores of their culture, sparks can fly. If your character

is closely tied to a particularly restrictive culture, consider how her personal morality is influenced by it.

In her 1989 coming-of-age novel, *The Floating World*, Cynthia Kadohata describes narrator Olivia's first time with a more ordinary boyfriend named Tan, who works with her at a chicken hatchery in Arkansas. They are both sixteen and have been necking and petting in an abandoned bus in the hatchery yard, thrilled by the possibility of being caught. Olivia is illegitimate, and she has grown up acutely conscious of the sexual arrangements and feelings of her mother and stepfather, her grandmother and other adults, so that she is open to her own sexuality.

When Olivia and Tan plan quite matter-of-factly to make love, they go to his parents' empty house, intending to use their bed. What Olivia has been reading recently in her grandmother's diaries is on her mind and part of her motivation to make love. In addition to her three husbands, Grandmother had seven lovers. About one of them she wrote that when they argued, she felt strong. Olivia realizes that more than wanting to feel love, she wants to feel the same strength her grandmother felt in the presence of a man.

Olivia and Tan end up in Tan's bed, kissing under the covers. Before long, Olivia panics about soiling the sheets and insists they move to the bathroom floor. Reluctantly Tan agrees, but once they get there and she lies down on the cold, hard tiles, she wants to go back to the bed:

> "Let's just stay," he said, breathing hard.
> "Well, okay." I closed my eyes as tightly as I could. "I'm ready," I said bravely. When nothing happened, I opened my eyes.
>
> He looked at me as if he had amnesia. Then he looked surprised, then frustrated. "Okay, okay," he said, half pulling me up. We stood and I saw his erection and was so surprised I walked into the doorjamb on the way out. When we got in bed I was surprised how ready I was, and how easily he slipped in. He moved in and out hard at first, making my head hit against the headboard. I wouldn't have minded, except I was scared I might get knocked out, and then I'd miss the most important part; but that didn't happen.

I expected that afterward I would feel some emotion re-
lated to love, and I did, but I also had a peculiar feeling a
shade shy of self-confidence.

When first-time lovers are young and living at home, the question
of *where* to do the deed is all important. Kadohata exploits this element and makes the actual place a source of humor and conflict
between Olivia and Tan.

Both Olivia's nervousness and her enthusiasm are essential to the
appeal of the scene. Let's look at how both work.

Olivia's nervous need to keep moving creates action and conflict.
Had Olivia and Tan kept kissing under the covers with one predictable thing leading to another, we would have had a much less lively
scene. Kadohata makes Olivia so nervous that she insists on playing
musical beds and floors. Her boyfriend, much more aroused than
she is and less concerned about leaving evidence, challenges her but
gives in every time. This gentle, innocent tension between them gives
the scene an element of conflict. It also reveals Olivia's nervousness
through her actions rather than through direct statements about her
state of mind.

Olivia's nervousness is a counterpoint to her enthusiasm. Her
plucky openness to the experience makes a nice contrast to her
jangling nerves. Had Kadohata dwelled on the nervousness without
injecting so much of Olivia's enthusiasm, the scene would have been
much flatter. Ironically, Olivia thinks she is motivated to make love
by wanting some of her grandmother's strength but as we see in this
scene, she already has plenty of self-confidence and a clear idea of
what she wants.

Molly Bolt, the tough, feisty narrator of Rita Mae Brown's *Rubyfruit
Jungle*, published in 1973, did for lesbian rights what *Fear of Flying*
would do that same year for the female orgasm: We had no choice
but to pay attention. In sixth grade, Molly proposes marriage to a
girl called Leota, whose own plans for her life at that point turn out
to be remarkably prescient. "I'll get married and have six children
and wear an apron like my mother, only my husband will be handsome." In the meantime, Leota is very keen on kissing Molly, and
more. During a sleep-over date, they finish watching Milton Berle

on television, shut the bedroom door, kiss for hours, and take off their pajamas:

> It was much better without the pajamas. I could feel her cool skin all over my body. That really was a lot better. Leota started kissing me with her mouth open. Now my stomach was going to fall out on the floor. . . . We kept on. . . . She began to touch me all over and I knew I was really going to die. Leota was bold. She wasn't afraid to touch anything and where her knowledge came from was a secret but she knew what she was after. And I soon found out.
>
> The next morning we went to school like any two sixth-grade girls.

Molly's wide-eyed openness to these events is in keeping with her already advanced sexual adventures: Until she was caught, she ran a nickel-a-look business, parading the uncircumcised penis of her friend Broccoli. But this night with Leota isn't business; it's her first sexual experience as a girl who will grow up to love women.

Soon after that first night, Molly's family moves away and the friends are separated until 1968 when Molly, now a student of film-making at NYU and what she calls a "devil-may-care lesbian," visits Leota in their hometown. Leota is married, has two kids, and at twenty-four, looks forty-five. When Molly asks if she ever thinks of that night, Leota says,

> "I'm too busy for that stuff. Who has time to think? Anyway, that was perverted, sick. I haven't got time for it. . . . Why did you ask me that? Why'd you come back here—to ask me that? You must have stayed that way. Is that why you're walking around in jeans and a pullover? You one of those sickies? . . . a pretty girl like you. You could have lots of men. You have more choices than I did here in this place."

When characters who have a same-sex first time in childhood meet again in adulthood and one or both have grown up to be gay, the early scene can take on a significance it might not have had for the characters at that time.

Alternatively, for gay characters or young people with homosexual feelings, a same-sex first time can be a major event in which characters feel not only sexually satisfied but relieved and liberated from the tyranny of trying to conform to a sexuality that doesn't fit.

For the fourteen-year-old boy called Ed in Edmund White's story, "Reprise," there are two distinct categories of "first times"—the technical first time and the first time that matters. "Until now," he tells us, "the people I'd had sex with were boys at camp who pretended to hypnotize each other or married men who cruised the Howard Street Elevated toilets and drove me down to the beach in station wagons filled with their children's toys."

But when, in 1954, Ed falls for Jim Grady, the college-age son of the man his mother is dating, he experiences the generous sex and affection of a man less inclined to lead a double life. The two boys connive to spend the night together at Ed's house, after watching the Perry Como show with Ed's mother. Jim feigns drunkenness and insists on sleeping over, rather than drive home in his condition. In Ed's room, where there is an extra bed,

> He lay back with a heavy-lidded, cool expression I suspected was patterned on Como's, but I didn't care, I was even pleased he wanted to impress me as I scaled his body, felt his great warm arms around me, tasted the Luckies and Bud on his lips. . . . "Hey," he whispered, and he smiled at me as his hands cupped my twenty-six inch waist and my hot penis planted its flag on the stony land of his perfect body. "Hey," he said, hitching me higher and deeper into his presence.

The surprise here for the reader is the significance of the single word "Hey" to the young narrator. Ironically, in this slight utterance Ed finds acceptance, intimacy and affection, different from what he found with boys and men who hid their desires with hypnotism and family life. "Jim was the first man who took off his clothes, held me in his arms, looked me in the eye, and said, 'Hey.' " Though he does not describe his encounters with these other men, we have to assume, from the weight he gives to "Hey," that they were starkly anonymous; that his partners were so uncomfortable with what they were doing that they could not even look at him, much less offer a mild endearment. As a result of Ed and Jim's brief association, Ed's mother discovers his homosexuality. His father is told, he is sent to a psychiatrist and to boarding school: "My entire life changed."

Forty years later the two men meet in a Paris hotel room: "When he hitched me into his embrace and said, 'Hey,' I felt fourteen again." The men's bodies have broadened and withered with age, but the nostalgic repetition of this single word is a kind of aphrodisiac.

- Intimacy can be conveyed in very small packages, in words of one syllable.
- Don't be shy about letting your first-time lovers meet again in adulthood. They won't all turn out to be like Leota from *Rubyfruit Jungle*.

In writing the sex scenes in my coming-of-age novel, *The Beginner's Book of Dreams*, I did not consciously try to create conflict or to inject surprises into the encounters, but rereading them now, I see how important those elements are, not only to the moments when flesh meets flesh but to everything that leads up to and follows them. As I wrote the chapter called "Staying Afloat," in which my sixteen-year-old main character, Esme Singer, loses her virginity, I was conscious of wanting to capture the roller coaster of emotions that comes with adolescence and with Esme's in particular, and the unusual sexual pressures and possibilities that arose in the late '60s and early '70s.

It's 1970 in New York City. Esme's boyfriend is Gene; her best friend is Leah. Esme's parents have been divorced since she was a young child. Her father is absent and full of promises he doesn't keep; as sexual mores loosen up, Esme's oft-married alcoholic mother turns to live-in boyfriends instead. Esme is, at once, emotionally resilient, high strung, and riven with self-doubt. The chapter opens like this:

> Three months of teenage sex, anguish. After school, their eyes closed, his younger brothers and sister barging into the room. Titters, confessions, terrible quarrels. Bare skin. Pleas for more, for restraint, the discovery of new languages, one for pleasure, one for denial. She would do everything but that. And that.
>
> "How can you be so prim and proper?" Gene asked. "You, of all people." They lay on her bed one afternoon with their shirts off, their legs entwined. "Your mother's living with Tommy Troy, and every time you call your father a different woman answers the phone. Do you think they're playing

chess?. . . Twelve-year-olds are screwing in Central Park, Leah's parents have a dinner-time discussion about the blow job in *Portnoy's Complaint*, and you've decided to be a virgin forever.''

"Not forever, just until—''

"I know, you're trying to be different from your parents.''

"Not just that. Leah and I—''

"Oh yes, your famous pact with Leah.''

"It's not just a pact, it's just that we're not going to sleep around. We're going to be different.''

"Sleeping with me isn't exactly sleeping around.''

Soon after, Gene, a senior in high school, learns he's been accepted at Harvard. He and Esme quarrel about whether they'll see each other once he leaves. Gene is angry with her for always berating herself and complaining about her parents.

". . . You think you're the only one in the world who got a crummy deal. Who has a fucked-up family!''

"I am!'' She dropped her book bag, pressed the coat against her face and cried into it.

He walked over to her and put his arms around her, nuzzled the coat away from her face. It fell to the floor between them.

"I'll do it now,'' she sputtered, and wiped her eyes with the back of her hand.

"What?'' He had not heard her.

"I'll do it now,'' she said more clearly.

"Do what?''

"You know.'' Her voice was hoarse, thick from crying.

He held her tighter. Her face was wet, her forehead sweaty. "Not now. . . .''

"Do you still want to?''

"Of course. But not now. . . .''

She turned her head and kissed him, felt him flinch, kissed him harder, deeper. He shook his head, tried gently to twist it away from her mouth. "I thought you liked that,'' she murmured.

"I do.''

She reached for his pants, his belt.

"Esme."

She licked his lips. "What."

"Don't."

"But you're so hard. Look." She unzipped his pants, she looked down, stroked him the way he liked, the way that made him breathe hard.

He looked down too and began to thrust gently. "Tighter," he said.

"Step back."

He stepped back, fell against the narrow bed. "The door's not locked."

"No one's home, are they?"

"Lock it. . . ."

Once they undress:

She lay down next to him and opened her mouth, gave him her tongue. She felt so warm underneath him, her legs opened wide. She did not know if it had started yet, if it was really there. "Put me in." She shook her head. He reached down between them. It was his fingers she felt now, in and out. Or maybe this was it. It did not hurt like it was supposed to. It did not feel like anything, but it did not feel like anything else. Then she began to cry out. He covered her mouth with his. She knew it would hurt the first time, but not like this.

Afterward, she asked, "Was it all right, was it good?"

"Yeah. . . ."

The smell of skin, sweat, sex. She closed her eyes and tried to separate it from the others. Yes, that was it. There and gone and then back again, like warm spots in a cold swimming pool.

"Look, we can't keep doing this," he said and took his arm from her. . . . "It wouldn't be right. . . . It's not what I want."

"Maybe you'll change your mind. You changed it just now."

"I won't. I've already decided."

As I look back on these scenes, I see that the characters are continually surprising one another with demands, insights or changes of heart. When Esme refuses to make love with Gene, he doesn't shut down and roll over; he challenges her. In challenging her, he not only forces her to fight back and defend her position, adding to the conflict between them, but he also reveals information to the reader about Esme's family, Leah's family, and the sexual attitudes of the times.

When she decides she wants to make love, he surprises her by not being interested. She doesn't back off, and she goes farther than he did when he refused; she manhandles him into submission. He then surprises her again by reverting to his original decision to break up with her.

None of these surprises is gratuitous; they are motivated by each character's needs, by the uncertainty and confusion of adolescence, and by the obstacles each character throws up to the other.

These are emotionally complex scenes in which sex plays predictable and then less predictable roles. We see clearly that sexual power is transitory, and the feelings of intimacy and closeness it brings are too.

LAST WORDS ABOUT THE FIRST TIME

If sex between first-time lovers isn't likely to secure them a listing in the *Guinness Book of World Records*, it is nevertheless a good place for you to begin to create compelling sex scenes. Why? Because what makes a first-time sex scene successful is what makes *all* good sex scenes work. As you write and rewrite, remember:

- A sex scene is not a sex manual for beginners. Stay with your characters' internal and external struggles, not only with their physical urges.
- Set up conflicts, obstacles and surprises for your characters that spring from who they are and their circumstances at the time.
- Integrate some or all of the given circumstances into the specific moment, or create a universe in which expectations are so different that the usual given circumstances do not apply.
- If a sex scene feels obligatory or gratuitous, leave it out or rewrite it to make it essential to the story or to our understanding of the characters.

CHAPTER SIX

Life Sentences

Husbands and Wives

BEN: You generally have the taste to let me *raise the subject of my ruined marriage.*
JOEY: I can't help wondering whether you miss it.
BEN: Only the sex and violence.

—Simon Gray, *Butley*

S leeping with the same person every night for years means you have moved "out of the gutter of wild desire onto the smooth lawns of married love," as English novelist Fay Weldon said in her novel *The Life and Loves of a She-Devil.* But take heart: *Writing* about married sex can be every bit as thrilling as creating a torrid encounter between lovers who have yearned for each other across decades.

What could possibly generate so much excitement for a writer? The whole thicket of circumstances that in real life makes married sex predictable and familiar also gives you material from which to create conflict, expectations, disappointments, surprises—in other words, plenty of drama. If the couple has children, you have a built-in source of tension and intrigue. It can be almost as much fun as writing about committing adultery: *Do we have time before they wake up? Will they hear? Oh no, that's Susie at the foot of the bed.*

But with or without children, your married characters have a sexual routine. When you lead them into bed together, don't forget that, as predictable as their moves might be to each other, they also have secrets, fantasies, desires, fears and other distractions that they keep to themselves—and that *you* are in a unique position to let us in on. In real life, a lover's distraction can be a hindrance to intimacy, but in fiction, distractions can lead to conflict, misunderstandings, unrealistic expectations, and large and small disappointments. These are gems to be mined and polished.

And because married people share so much of life beyond sex, the rest of life can easily creep into their thoughts and deeds while making love, so that a sex scene can become a snapshot—more like a Polaroid—of a couple's life together.

This is certainly the case in a scene, too long to be included here, from chapter one of John Updike's *Rabbit is Rich.* After twenty years of marriage, Toyota dealer Harry Angstrom is more interested in reading *Consumer Reports* than in his drunken wife's advances. Once Harry relents and tosses aside the magazine, Janice tries to arouse him, but what gets him going are memories of a girl from ninth grade and a lover for whom he briefly left Janice many years before. Their few lines of dialogue are sadly revealing of the distance between them. Before their lovemaking goes too far, Janice passes out, though Harry is now aroused. He rearranges her body and decides to enter her from behind, so that "his prick is stiff as stone inside a sleeping woman. . . . Love has lulled her, liquor has carried her off. Bless that dope. . . . He is stealthy so as not to wake her but single in his purpose, quick, and pure." A sex scene between Harry and Janice Angstrom is a mini-history of their unhappy marriage.

In *Presumed Innocent* Scott Turow's narrator Rusty Sabitch spells out the limitations and burdens of married sex—the weight of history, all those quotidian distractions—by way of explaining his attraction to Carolyn Polhemus, whose murder he is charged with committing: "After almost twenty years of sleeping with Barbara, I no longer went to bed with only her. I lay down with five thousand other fucks; with the recollection of younger bodies; with the worries for the million things that supported and surrounded our life."

In these days of boundless sexual openness, an author's reticence can be more revealing than it was when *everyone* had to keep quiet about sex. In *Light Years*, his luminous novel about the slow disintegration of what seems like an ideal marriage, James Salter makes an inaudible comment about the state of Viri and Nedra's sex life. In separate highly erotic scenes, we see both husband and wife make love with their respective lovers, but when they get into bed with each other, it is only to go to sleep.

Other fictional married couples, like many real ones, go to great lengths to keep their passions aflame, but none, I think, does it more ambitiously than the couple in Peruvian writer Mario Vargas Llosa's novel, *In Praise of the Stepmother*. Husband and wife are nightly aroused by telling their own erotic versions of classic myths based on well-known paintings. A glossy print of each painting is included in the novel, a sly gesture by the author: Not only does he want us to see what inspires his characters, but he's inviting us to invent our own erotic tales.

GIVEN CIRCUMSTANCES

1. The characters have a complex shared history.
2. There is no drama inherent in married sex. People are usually not worried about being caught or leaving evidence, about who might have seen them enter the building and how much time they have left. In theory anyway, married sex is always available.
3. Couples may have a sexual routine, or go through cycles of passion, tenderness, distraction or alienation. In any case, they are not likely to surprise one another with revelations about their sexuality or circumstances.
4. Nevertheless, they may have secrets, fantasies and desires they keep to themselves.
5. Because they share so much of life beyond sex, the rest of life can easily creep into their thoughts *and* deeds while making love, as when Harry Angstrom can't stop reading *Consumer Reports* in *Rabbit is Rich*.
6. Characters very likely feel comfortable and unself-conscious with one another.
7. Characters with children may worry about waking them, or being disturbed or inhibited by them.

EXAMPLES

In this scene from Toni Morrison's *The Bluest Eye*, Pauline tells the erotic history of her marriage in a stream-of-consciousness style that seems closer to jazz or abstract painting than chronological narrative. She recalls, almost relives, the powerful but bittersweet sex she and husband Cholly had in the days before his chronic drunkenness. Now that she has two children and understands Cholly cannot support them, she has become a serious churchgoer and breadwinner, "an ideal servant," in the words of her rich, white employers whose house—unlike her own—is a source of pride to her. Occasionally she allows herself the pleasure of remembering those nights with Cholly:

> *He used to come easing into bed sometimes, not too drunk. I make out like I'm asleep, 'cause it's late, and he taken three dollars out of my pocketbook that morning or something. . . . I think about the thick, knotty hair on his chest, and the two big swells his breast muscles make. . . . I pretend to wake up, and turn to him, but not opening my legs. I want him to open them for me. He does, and I be soft and wet where his fingers are strong and hard. I be softer than I ever been before. All my strength in his hand. My brain curls up like wilted leaves. . . . I stretch my legs open, and he is on top of me. Too heavy to hold, and too light not to. He puts his thing in me. In me. In me. I wrap my feet around his back so he can't get away. His face is next to mine. The bed springs sounds like them crickets used to back home. He puts his fingers in mine, and we stretches our arms outwise like Jesus on the cross. I hold on tight. My fingers and my feet hold on tight, because everything else is going, going. I know he wants me to come first. But I can't. Not until he does. Not until I feel him loving me. Just me. Sinking into me. Not until I know that my flesh is all that be on his mind. That he couldn't stop if he had to. That he would die rather than take his thing out of me. Of me. Not until he has let go of all he has, and give it to me. To me. To me. When he does, I feel a power. I be strong, I be pretty, I be young. And then I wait. He shivers and tosses his head. Now I be strong enough, pretty enough, and young enough to let him make me come. I take my fingers out of his and put my hands on his behind. My legs drop back onto the bed. I don't make no noise, because the chil'ren might hear. I begin to feel those little bits of color floating up into me—deep in me. That streak of green from the june-bug light, the purple from the berries trickling along my thighs, Mama's lemonade yellow runs sweet in me. Then I feel like I'm laughing between my legs, and the laughing gets all mixed up with the colors, and I'm afraid I'll come, and afraid I won't. But I know I will. And I do. And it be rainbow all inside. And it lasts and lasts and lasts. I want to thank him, but don't know*

how, so I pat him like you do a baby. He asks me if I'm all right. I
say yes. He gets off me and lies down to sleep. I want to say something,
but I don't. I don't want to take my mind offen the rainbow.

As in Molly Bloom's stream-of-consciousness soliloquy in James
Joyce's *Ulysses*, Morrison's presentation of Pauline's memories attempts to mimic her mental process, so we experience her thoughts
and feelings with a startling immediacy. The intensity of Pauline and
Cholly's sexual connection almost makes up for all they can't say to
each other in words. But it is Pauline's awareness of the distance
between them—at first, when she's pretending to be asleep and afterwards, when she doesn't want to speak—that helps give this scene its
melancholy edge. Even Pauline's fondest memories of making love
with Cholly are tinged with disappointment.

One of the great pleasures of this passage for me is its varieties of
language. Morrison mixes sexual bluntness and no-nonsense detail—
I be soft and wet; he puts his thing in me; he wants me to come first—with
lyrical metaphors, figures of speech, invented words and religious
references that transport us beyond the realm of purely physical
sensation:

> *My brain curls up like wilted leaves.*
> *The bed springs sounds like them crickets used to back home. . . .*
> *. . . we stretches our arms outwise like Jesus on the cross.*
> *those little bits of color floating up into me—deep in me.*
> *Then I feel like I'm laughing between my legs, and the laughing*
> *gets all mixed up with the colors.*
> *And it be a rainbow all inside.*

Read the passage again and then refer back to the list of given
circumstances. How many of the general truths about married sex
has Morrison incorporated into this scene? How has she made them
specific to Pauline and Cholly's lives?

Dick and May Pierce, in John Casey's *Spartina*, are not afflicted
with an excess of desire for one another. Their long marriage is
strained and beset with money problems. In this scene, Dick, a Rhode
Island fisherman, has news on his mind he does not tell May about
the fishing boat he is building. In the chapter immediately after this,
Dick takes a lover, Elsie, who will help get him money to build the

boat. His keeping a business secret from May foreshadows the more threatening secret he is soon to have.

Early one morning Dick comes home from a several-day-long fishing trip. May greets him, offers him breakfast and, when he declines, she makes a sexual proposition so noncommittal and dreary we might mistake it for small talk: "Well," she says, "why don't you go ahead and take your shower. The boys are out for the morning. I was going to clean some, but I can get to it later." Then:

> He showered, came out in his towel, and took a hold of May's long waist. On the bed he slid her hairpins out the way she liked, even slower than usual, so it got to her more than usual, but all the while he couldn't get his mind off how he couldn't tell her what was going on on account of how right she'd been about Parker. He rubbed her slip on her skin the way she liked, feeling indecently competent as she breathed harder and got pink and hypnotized.
>
> Later on she said that she'd forgotten how much she used to miss him when he'd been going out regular on a boat. It was a nice thing to say, but it didn't reach him. He looked up at a thin spattering of rain across the windowpane, the tired southwester dragging on.

Most of the given circumstances of married sex apply here, all of them filtered through the lens of Dick and May's routine coupling. Their sexual pattern is down pat; seduction has been reduced to "I was going to clean but I can do it later." Once they begin, Dick uses several familiar gestures to arouse her. Rather than being carried away, all he feels is "indecently competent." Even the gloomy weather he notices out the window afterwards reinforces the emotional staleness between them. And of course, he's distracted by the secret he is keeping from her about the boat. Casey makes this sexual encounter with May important to the novel because it reveals to us the uninspired state of their intimacy, so that we are not surprised when Dick is susceptible to Elsie's entreaties in the next chapter.

This scene is a reminder to connect sex scenes to the total package of your characters' needs and wants and to the larger story, so that scenes do not feel "dropped in" and gratuitous. Because Dick's infatuation with Elsie is so central to *Spartina*, it is important we see the limitations of his sex life with his wife.

For couples with small children, married sex is often the sex that almost was—The Sex That Got Away. So it is for Lewis and Katie in Ron Carlson's short story, "Plan B for the Middle Class." Married for fourteen years, they haven't had much sex since their sons were born three years before. At last, they're leaving the kids with grandparents for a few days and heading for Hawaii: "I am one revolution of the earth away from the most astonishing sex carnival ever staged by two married people," narrator Lewis tells us. The only trouble is he has just been fired from his lucrative job writing a syndicated column on animal life (fundamentalist hate mail against evolution did him in), he hasn't told his wife yet, and he's got a nasty case of jock itch.

The night before they leave for Hawaii, they attempt a dress rehearsal for the carnival:

> The length of her body is the simple answer to what I am missing. It's an odd sensation to have something in your arms and to still be yearning for it and you lie there and feel the yearning subside slowly as the actual woman rises along your neck, chest, legs. We are drifting against each other now. Sex is the raft, but sleep is the ocean and the waves are coming up. . . . I run my hands along her bare back and down across her ribs and feel the two dimples in her hip and my only thought is the same thought I've had a thousand times: I don't remember this—I don't remember this at all.
>
> Katie sits up and places her warm legs on each side of me, her breasts falling forward in the motion, and as she lifts herself ever so slightly in a way that is the exact synonym for losing my breath, we see something.
>
> There is a faint movement in our room, and Katie ducks back to my chest.

Their little boy is at the door, a reminder that there can be plenty of drama—great expectations dashed by the patter of little feet—in a sex scene between husbands and wives.

Once Katie and Lewis get to Hawaii, there are no children underfoot but Carlson sets up enough obstacles, conflicts and surprises—everything from a giant panda to a pair of young widows—to keep them from even being in the same room together for another twenty-three pages. Close to midnight, the carnival finally gets going:

Now this next part, the bodies roll, their design made manifest, and there is achieved a radical connection. I'm not talking about souls. Who can tell about this stuff? Not me. You're there, you are both in something, something carnal and vaporish at once. Your mouths cock half a turn and you sense the total lock. You're transferring brains here; your spine glows. You go to heaven and right through, there's no stopping. What do you call it? Fucking? Not quite right here, this original touch, the firmament. My credo: you enter and she takes you in. This is personal. This is cooperation. Who can live to tell about it? You cooperate until you're married cell to cell, until all words flash away in the dark.

Lewis had promised us, and himself, an X-rated love fest, but what we get here instead is an astonishing piece of writing on the impossibility of describing sex and on its peculiar, total and elemental power. If surprises are essential to a good sex scene, one of Carlson's surprises here is how much the passage is about *ideas of sex*. His goal here isn't to put us inside his character's skin but to put us inside his head as he grapples with the conundrum of sex, with what sex is and isn't and what it should be called. Afterwards his wife is sated and falls asleep immediately, but Lewis is up for hours more, wandering the hotel and the beach, remembering his high school graduation and the girl he was supposed to lose his virginity with that night. His Hawaiian sex carnival has become a history lesson in his own evolution, tying it to the human history of evolution, and those fundamentalists who try to deny it, and who cost him his job as a columnist.

> • Because married sex partners are so familiar to one another, because they are not making fresh physical discoveries the way new lovers are, a sex scene can have a more ruminative quality. While making love, a character has the luxury to wonder about the meanings and mysteries of the sexual connection.

The Stone Diaries, which won the Pulitzer Prize for Fiction in 1995, is the inventive, collagelike diary of Daisy Stone Flett, an orphan whose life spans the twentieth century. Made up of eighty years of diary entries in the first and third person, letters, photographs, and short-story-like narratives, Mrs. Flett reveals the sad truth about her sex life with her husband in a chapter called "Motherhood, 1947," under a heading she calls "Mrs. Flett's Intimate Relations with her Husband." Because she "deeply, fervently, sincerely" wants to be a good wife and mother, she reads every issue of *McCalls* and *Good Housekeeping*, which even in 1947 are crammed with advice and letters from readers on sex. One reader asks if her husband's desire for sex every night is normal, leading Daisy to think:

> ". . . every night" would be a lot to put up with. Neverthe-less she always prepares herself, just in case—her diaphragm in position, though she is repelled by its yellow look of decay and the cold, slick-smelling jelly she smears around its edges. It's a bother, and nine times out of ten it isn't needed, but it seems this is something that has to be put up with.

Mrs. Flett expects to perform her marital duties on nights before her husband leaves on business trips ("as a sort of vaccination, she sometimes thinks") and when he returns. Here she imagines what might take place upon his imminent return after he has removed his trousers and tie:

> Then, unaware of her tears wetting the blanket binding and the depth of her loneliness this September night, he will lie down on top of her, being careful not to put too much weight on her frame ("A gentleman always supports himself on his elbows"). His eyes will be shut, and his warm penis will be produced and directed inside her, and then there will be a few minutes of rhythmic rocking.
>
> On and on it will go while Mrs. Flett tries, as through a helix of mixed print and distraction, to remember exactly what was advised in the latest issue of *McCalls*, something about a wife's responsibility for demonstrating a rise in ardor.

These passages are great fun to read, full of period-piece detail, lovely juxtapositions and unexpected sadness. They are excellent ex-amples of how a sex scene, or an imagined scene, can reveal a great deal about character (Mrs. *and* Mr. Flett) and the sexual attitudes of the period. They reveal all this in a lively, original voice (Mrs. Flett's, being self-mocking), using details that locate us in the historical period and in the emotional desert Mrs. Flett wants to escape—but certainly won't, given the powers lined up against her (her husband

and *Good Housekeeping* both). The passages and the period bring to mind Carolyn See's right-between-the-eyes line in her novel *Golden Days*: "I am speaking to you of the days when men did push-ups on your body and called that sex."

There are many events and circumstances that alter a married couple's sexual routine—altering the given circumstances as well—but none is more profound than the death or disappearance of a child, who exists, after all, because of this intimacy. A child missing, dead or in serious trouble falls at the far end of a spectrum of child-related disturbances that can have powerful effects on a couple's sex life: everything from an infant's first fever to a teenager's first date.

Let's look at what happens in two recent novels in which parents have absent children too much on their minds.

In British writer Ian McEwan's *The Child in Time*, the loving marriage of Stephen and Julie Lewis shatters soon after their three-year-old daughter is stolen from a London supermarket during a few seconds when her father turned away from her. The child is never found; the parents separate. Stephen turns to drink and Julie to mysticism. She moves to the country and two years later, while he is visiting her after a long absence, they end up in the bed that had been a wedding gift:

> The homely and erotic patterns of marriage are not easily discarded. They knelt face to face in the center of the bed undressing each other slowly.
>
> "You're so thin," said Julie. "You're going to waste away." She ran her hands along the pole of his collarbone, down the bars of his ribcage, and then, gratified by his excitement, held him tight in both hands and bent down to reclaim him with a long kiss.
>
> He too felt proprietorial tenderness once she was naked. He registered the changes, the slight thickening at the waist, the large breasts a little smaller. From living alone, he thought, as he closed his mouth around the nipple of one and pressed the other against his cheek. The novelty of seeing and feeling a familiar naked body was such that for some minutes they could do little more than hold each other at arm's length and say, "Well . . ." and "Here we are

again. . . ." A wild jokiness hung in the air, a suppressed hilarity that threatened to obliterate desire. . . .

He wondered, as he had many times before, how anything so good and simple could be permitted, how they were allowed to get away with it, how the world could have taken this experience into account for so long and still be the way it was. Not governments or publicity firms or research departments, but biology, existence, matter itself had dreamed this up for its own pleasure and perpetuity, and this was exactly what you were meant to do, it wanted you to like it.

When their seventeen-year-old son Jacob is accused of murdering his girlfriend, Carolyn and Ben Reiser's world is permanently altered in Rosellen Brown's novel *Before and After*, a dramatic exploration of a parent's duty to shield a child from the consequences of his crime. The boy flees their small New England town and is apprehended months later in Cambridge, Massachusetts. After a chilling family reunion at the jail, during which Jacob does not say a word, Carolyn and Ben spend the night with friends in Cambridge—a successful couple with young children, a beautiful house, and a maid who cooks exotic meals. Since the police first came looking for their son, Carolyn and Ben have not made love. Late that night in the guest bedroom:

> His hands were everywhere on her, every part of him awake and anxious. He didn't say a word.
>
> She didn't resist. Confused, not sure whether this was a violation or his reading of a need of hers more secret than even she could acknowledge, she let him chafe her skin pink under his rough carpenter's hands and lay her back across the edge of the bed, where he pinned her desperately to the pink-and-green garlands on the sheets. He took no time with her, so that he had to rip his way in, and he howled when he came. He sounded like a man felled from behind by surprise.

She imagines the child in the next room hearing the howl and fearing that "someone—someone else" was being murdered. She moves away from her husband, glares at him, and says, "What a performance." She then accuses him of making so much noise as a way to assert himself, because over dinner the man of the house had been knowing and certain as to how they should handle their legal problems. Ben answers:

"You think that, hunh?" He closed his eyes and swayed a
little like a man at prayer. "Won't anything ever be the same
again? Carolyn? This will sound sentimental, I know, but—
we're here in this—this normal house. I see these two people
who can get into bed together at the end of the day like ordinary people and enjoy each other, make love like—friends,
whatever you want to call it—and then turn over and go to
sleep and not have dreams with battered heads in them and
see the straps of electric chairs. . . . So I looked at the two of
them, those two fucking lucky people, and I thought, That's
what they're going to do when they go to bed tonight, they're
going to think about us, poor schmucks who are in such
trouble, and they're going to reach out for each other and
celebrate their good luck. So I reached for you. So. I'm
sorry."

When writing about a couple in these circumstances, keep in mind
that the loss of a child is so powerful and consuming, you may not
even have to mention it directly to make the reader experience the
characters' anguish.

What separates a sex scene between characters with these burdens
from other married characters?

- The couples' ordinary sexual routine has been so profoundly
disturbed that when they do make love, it's a kind of "first time"
for them. They are full of insights about the nature of sex (as in
The Child in Time) or disturbing observations about their long-time
partner (*Before and After*).
- They are in a heightened state of awareness, which is atypical
of married sex.
- Sex now includes an element of drama—the missing child,
the child in trouble—also atypical of married sex.
- It may also include feelings of guilt, ordinarily not associated
with married sex: guilt at the pleasure they feel while their child
may be in danger, guilt that they have not managed to protect the
child. Pleasure becomes a kind of betrayal of loyalty to the child.

Then there are the innocent pleasures of prospective parenthood.
This passage from John Cheever's classic first novel, *The Wapshot
Chronicle*, published in 1957—a little too early for explicit sex between

married characters—includes a delightful *reference* to married sex in the context of the romantic, affectionate evening on which Coverly Wapshot learns his wife Betsey is pregnant. After dinner she wants to go shopping for a chair in which to nurse their child. The passage conveys a degree of enthusiasm for sex atypical of the fiction of the period and leaves us with a very strong sense of the tenor of the sex and the cozy state of intimacy between husband and wife:

> After supper they took their walk. A fresh wind was blowing out of the north—straight from St. Botolphs—and it made Betsey feel vigorous and gay. She took Coverly's arm and at the corner, under the fluorescent street lamp, he bent down and gave her a French kiss. Once they got to the shopping center Betsey wasn't able to concentrate on her chair. Every suit, dress, fur coat and piece of furniture in the store windows had to be judged, its price and way of life guessed at and some judgment passed as to whether or not it should enter Betsey's vision of happiness. Yes, she said to a plant stand, yes, yes to a grand piano, no to a breakfront, yes to a dining-room table and six chairs, as thoughtfully as Saint Peter sifting out the hearts of men. At ten o'clock they walked home. Coverly undressed her tenderly and they took a bath together and went to bed for she was his potchke, his fleutchke, his notchke, his motchke, his everything that the speech of St. Botolphs left unexpressed. She was his little, little squirrel.

LAST WORDS ABOUT MARRIED SEX

The sex lives of married characters were strictly off-limits in fiction until the 1960s. Even D.H. Lawrence, who wrote explicitly about adultery in *Lady Chatterley's Lover*, and sex between men and women who were not married in *Women in Love*, didn't reveal a thing about what went on between husbands and wives. The nineteenth-century European novels that shook with adulterous tremors—*Madame Bovary, Anna Karenina, The Red and the Black*—were silent about what went on in the marriage bed. Did authors keep mum because sex between their married but unfaithful characters was nonexistent, because it was uneventful compared to the extracurricular stuff, or because of a delicacy that honored the sacredness of marriage even as spouses violated their vows? Of course we will never know, but now that we have carte blanche to open the bedroom door on our married characters, we need more than ever to make it worth a reader's while. We know, after all, what goes on in there. It is the one place where sexual intimacy is officially sanctioned, where sex is *supposed* to happen. So the fact that it does is not particularly noteworthy, unless the author makes it so by creating a scene that tells us something essential about the nature of a couple's intimacy and what it has to do with the rest of the story.

CHAPTER SEVEN

Three Cheers for Adultery

"I am more attached to her—than I thought it possible to be to any woman after three years. . . . If Lady [Byron] would but please to die—and the Countess G's husband—(for Catholics can't marry though divorced) we should probably have to marry—though I would rather not—thinking it the way to hate each other."

—Lord Byron (in a letter to his sister, 1821)

I f adultery did not exist, writers would have had to invent it. It offers a sizzling spread of possibilities for conflict, high emotion, reversals of fortune, acts of moral turpitude, and sex that's too hot to handle. Better still, from the point of view of a writer who wants sparks to fly between more than two characters, a single act of infidelity can involve an epic and explosive cast: the two lovers, their cuckolded spouses, friends and colleagues privy to the deception, and unwitting, miscellaneous witnesses.

When writing about married sex, as we saw in chapter six, we often need to create tension and drama by plumbing the depths of our characters' psyches. But when the subject is infidelity, the drama is built into the encounter. Sometimes your best move can be to steer a hard course away from the predictable high emotion of it by creating characters who are blasé and unrepentant, as Tomas is about his chronic infidelities in Czech writer Milan Kundera's *The Unbearable Lightness of Being*. Another very male, very British approach is explored in *Betrayal*, a play by Harold Pinter later made into a wonderful movie with Ben Kingsley and Jeremy Irons. The men are good friends and colleagues and one is having an affair of long standing with the other's wife. The men go through elaborate rituals of friendship over many years by completely ignoring the dangerous current that surges between them. Talk about tension, talk about subtext!

What else can a writer do with all the potential melodrama of adultery? Leaven it with humor, irreverence and irony, as Joseph Heller does in *Something Happened*, in the excerpt later in this chapter. Or go whole hog, give in to the drama of it and take us for a roller coaster ride, as Scott Turow does in *Presumed Innocent*, in which the wife of a cheating husband kills his girlfriend and manages to frame her husband for the murder.

In real life we may want our two-timing spouses to renounce their lovers and take the high road to domestic harmony, but in fiction, where conflict is the catchword, it's far more compelling when they don't. There would have been no stories to tell had Flaubert's Emma Bovary made do with dreary Charles and Tolstoy's Anna Karenina settled for a pallid marriage. Two of my favorite adulterers in recent fiction are husbands who can't give up the habit. Milan Kundera's Tomas is "genuinely incapable of abandoning his erotic friendships" and goes home to his wife's bed every night with his hair reeking of sex. In Fay Weldon's dark, funny fairy tale, *The Life and Loves of a She-Devil*, Ruth's accountant husband Bobbo takes up with his client, Mary Fisher. Bobbo not only refuses to give Mary up, but insists on regaling Amazon-size Ruth with professions of love for petite Mary. His refusal to renounce Mary sets in motion Ruth's own wildly elaborate plan for revenge. Three cheers for adultery!—when it leads characters and authors to these heights of invention.

GIVEN CIRCUMSTANCES

1. The sex is preheated—charged by its very nature—because the lovers meet in secret; there's typically an element of danger in being seen together and a time limit on the meeting. Urgency and deception can fuel eros.
2. Adulterers live at least three lives: the public, the married, the illicit.
3. Adulterous sex is compartmentalized.

4. Adulterers often compare the lover to the spouse. Lovers may solicit comparisons.

5. Adulterers try to conceal evidence—lipstick, body odor, restaurant receipts, or subtle changes in behavior and attitudes.

6. Emotions run the gamut from exhilaration and liberation to shame and remorse.

7. The romantic triangle has an inherent source of tension. If both adulterous lovers have spouses, possibilities for conflict, communication and deception increase.

8. Desire for a person you can't have and don't know very well can take a long time to exhaust.

9. There's often an imbalance of power between adulterous lovers, with men usually in the lead. Society's double standards often judge cheating wives more harshly than cheating husbands. And with more married men than married women having affairs, men have more choices for partners than women do, again tipping the power in their favor.

10. Adultery is unpredictable, potentially explosive, and can lead easily to pain and dislocation for many—lovers, spouses and children.

And yet, and yet . . . for the writer, as well as for lovers new to the beat, adultery is as seductive, and sometimes as hard to kick, as nicotine. Here's how British sociologist Annette Lawson describes its power in a 1989 study called *Adultery*:

> Adultery, because it is secret, permits people endless variation. In adultery, each partner can make the lover represent anyone or anything—mother, father, sibling, superordinates or subordinates, angel or devil—with very little risk because, unlike marriage, adultery does not, at the outset, include permanence. Truth need never be revealed; the inadequacies of the reality of the self need never be demonstrated to the other. So long as the adultery is brief, the fantasy can endure. In this sense, adultery is far from dangerous; it is safe.

EXAMPLES

A character's attitude toward adultery, often a shadow image of society's view, can set the tone for an entire novel. When Anna Karenina and Vronsky finally become lovers, they are so riven by guilt and shame that he compares what they have done to committing murder.

These days, the power of shame to proscribe behavior isn't what it used to be. Mirroring society's attitudes, adulterous lovers who find their way to literature have little truck with the concept of remorse. For Bob Slocum, the amusingly tormented narrator of Joseph Heller's *Something Happened*, adultery is a fringe benefit of marriage. He even recommends it for his wife.

Though this monologue does not describe a sexual encounter, it illustrates how much mileage you can get out of giving your unfaithful characters well-defined attitudes towards adultery. In this case, Slocum's attitude is raunchy and irreverent, in keeping with Heller's tone throughout the novel.

> My wife is at that stage now where she probably *should* commit adultery—and would, if she had more character. It might do her much good. I remember the first time I committed adultery. (It wasn't much good.)
>
> "Now I'm committing adultery," I thought.
>
> It was not much different from the first time I laid my wife after we were married.
>
> "Now I am laying my wife," I thought.
>
> It would mean much more to her (I think), for I went into my marriage knowing I would commit adultery the earliest chance I had (it was a goal; committing adultery, in fact, was one of the reasons *for* getting married), while she did not (and probably has not really thought of it yet. It may be that I do all of the thinking about it for her.). I did not even give up banging the other girl I'd been sleeping with fairly regularly until some months afterward. I got four or five other girls up at least once those first two years also just to see for myself that I really could.
>
> I think I might really feel like killing my wife, though, if she did it with someone I know in the company. My wife has red lines around her waist and chest when she takes her clothes off and baggy pouches around the sides and bottom of her behind, and I would not want anyone I deal with in the company to find that out. (I would want them to see her only at her best. Without those red marks.)

The juiciest surprise of this passage—following a trail of bread-crumb-size surprises about his sexual past—is Slocum's reason for not wanting his wife to sleep with any of his colleagues. Heller sets up the surprise by having Slocum tell us first that he would feel like "killing her" if she slept with a colleague. We expect him to elaborate with something like, "I couldn't bear to share my wife with the vice president of marketing." But instead of garden variety jealousy, he surprises us with what he feels are the humiliating imperfections of her flesh. Even in his fantasy of her unfaithfulness, he wants to look good for the guys at work.

There is also some ambiguity in Slocum's remarks. Because this statement occurs late in the novel, we know by now to take his most intimate feelings with a grain of salt, to look for the ways in which he is not being entirely candid with us or himself. It suits his tough-guy image to assert that the only reason he doesn't want his wife to sleep with someone in the company is because it might make him look bad. It's safer for him to joke about her body than to admit it would hurt his feelings for her to sleep with someone else.

- Whether you convey it directly or by suggestion, give us a sense of how your adulterous characters feel about the trust they are betraying. Are they guilt-ridden, sarcastic and defensive, or— the untroubled few—blessedly content?

People who go to the trouble—and take the risk—of committing adultery understandably have high hopes for their assignations. The higher their hopes, the farther they have to fall when plans go awry. To the cheating lovers, mechanical failures or logistical impediments can be devastating, but to a writer interested in crafting a compelling sex scene, there's nothing like a lost car key or a little impotence to subvert the predictable.

In Erica Jong's *Fear of Flying*, her Rabelaisian heroine, Isadora Wing, has just come to "that inevitable year when fucking [your husband] turned as bland as Velveeta cheese." Rather than leave the marriage, she searches for an uncomplicated, anonymous fling, what she calls "the Zipless Fuck." Enter Adrian Goodlove, a British psychoanalyst Isadora meets while attending a convention of analysts in Vienna with her analyst husband Bennett. After necking with Adrian in a parking lot, Isadora is convinced he is a prime candidate—her first live wire—for a zipless dalliance. A day later, she's in his hotel room:

> In his room, I stripped naked in one minute flat and lay on the bed.
>
> "Pretty desperate, aren't you?" he asked.
>
> "Yes."
>
> "For God's sake, why? We have plenty of time."
>
> "How long?"
>
> "As long as you want it," he said, ambiguously. If he left me, in short, it would be my fault. Psychoanalysts are like that. Never fuck a psychoanalyst is my advice to all you young things out there.
>
> Anyway, it was no good. Or not much. He was only at half-mast and he thrashed around wildly inside me hoping I wouldn't notice. I wound up with a tiny ripple of an orgasm and a very sore cunt. But somehow I was pleased. I'll be able to get free of him now, I thought; he isn't a good lay. I'll be able to forget him.
>
> "What are you thinking?" he asked.
>
> "That I've been well and truly fucked." I remembered having used the same phrase with Bennett once, when it was much more true.
>
> "You're a liar and a hypocrite. What do you want to lie for? I know I haven't fucked you properly. I can do much better than that."
>
> I was caught up short by his candor. "OK," I confessed glumly, "you haven't fucked me properly. I admit it."

When she admits she had been afraid to be honest with him, he surprises her by saying that his ego isn't as fragile as she had imagined. When she says she has never met anyone like him, his answer is far from perfunctory: ". . . No, you haven't, ducks, and I daresay you never will again. I told you I'm an anti-hero. I'm not here to rescue you—and carry you away on a white horse." Is he being profound or just defensive because he couldn't perform? Whatever his motivation, his retort about not rescuing her on a white horse is germane to the rest of the novel and to her internal struggles: how Isadora can make peace with her desires for sex, love, fame, creative fulfillment, emotional security and independence. Adrian's offhand remarks throw the central issues of the novel back into her court in ways she could not have anticipated.

Like all true heroines, Isadora has decided what she wants, gone after it, been thwarted—and keeps on plugging. Her setback is only temporary. Even after this encounter with Adrian, she still wants to find bliss and transcendence with him; she won't quit for another two hundred pages.

After the brief paragraph that summarizes their disappointing sex—so unsatisfying that Jong just touches on the low points, rather than recreating each stroke—she skillfully keeps the scene going by making Adrian the dominant character, the character who does not accept Isadora's statements at face value and challenges every one of them, creating conflict and causing her to face up to her own dishonesty and her own illusions.

The scene turns on two surprises: First, a surprise of action: the zipless fuck can't get it up; second, a surprise of character: though Adrian has failed her test for potency, he has passed "a character test" she had not even meant to administer. Unlike Isadora, he is willing to talk honestly, take responsibility for his actions (and failures to act), and confront her with insights she would rather avoid.

Some of the tension and energy in this scene comes from the fact that Isadora and Adrian go to bed together with vastly different expectations. She is embarked on a major marital/psychic experiment; he is just looking for a good time. When the machinery doesn't work, he can say to himself, and to her, "Better luck next time." But for Isadora, the mechanical glitch shatters a fantasy she has counted on to rescue her from the doldrums of her marriage. It makes great sense that Adrian can bring insight and observation to the encounter that Isadora cannot: He sees it for what it is— a romp with a near stranger, not a magic potion for a woman in the midst of a crisis.

- Adultery is a high-stakes gamble in which both partners are not often satisfied equally because expectations and disappointments tend to run to extremes. Make sure at least one of your characters wants something very specific from the exchange, make sure we know by the end of the scene whether he or she has gotten it—and also what it might have cost him or her, in pride, self-esteem or sexual identity.

The mood is mournful and elegiac in this scene from Russell Banks' novel, *The Sweet Hereafter*. Narrator Billy Ansel, a young widower, is recalling everything that led up to the school bus accident in which his twins and twelve other local children were killed. His former lover Risa and her husband Wendell own a motel; their child was one of those killed. Before the accident, he and Risa met regularly in room eleven of her motel while a baby-sitter took care of his twins. The accident brought an end to the affair, but while it was going on he would sit in the dark motel room waiting for her:

> It sounds sordid, I know, but it didn't feel cheap or low. It was too often too lonely, too solitary, for that. Many nights Risa could not get away to Room 11, and I sat there by myself in the wicker chair beside the bed for an hour or so, smoking cigarettes and thinking and remembering my life before Lydia died, until finally, when it was clear that Risa could not get away from Wendell, I would leave the room and walk across the road to the lot next to the Rendez-Vous where I had parked my truck and drive home.
>
> On those nights when Risa did arrive, we spent our time together entirely in darkness, for we couldn't turn on the room light, and we barely saw each other, except for what we could make out in the dim light from the motel sign outside falling through the blinds: rose-colored profiles, the curve of a thigh or shoulder, a breast, a knee. It was melancholy and sweet and reflective, and of course very sexual, straight-forwardly sexual, for both of us.
>
> Our meetings were respites from our real and very troubled lives, and we knew that. Whenever I saw Risa in daylight, in public, it was as if she were a wholly different person, her sister, maybe, or a cousin, who only resembled in vague ways the woman I was having an affair with.

The loveliest and most instructive surprises of this scene are Banks' use of the motel and of the darkness, separate elements that he fuses together to great effect. Having Billy Ansel's married lover own a motel gives Banks the opportunity for the two to betray her husband on his own property, an extra-dangerous and extra-treacherous gesture.

The fact that Risa shows up sometimes and not others—and that

Billy waits in the dark for her—adds to the precariousness of the relationship, and the sadness. Looking back at the relationship through the prism of the accident and the children's deaths magnifies the sadness of the affair a thousandfold.

But what looms largest and most hauntingly in this scene is the darkness in which they make love, and the glancing slivers of light that illuminate disparate body parts. The darkness is a necessary part of their camouflage, but Banks uses it as almost another character in the scene—the character who gives them permission to have their straightforward sex with no emotional attachments or complications; they can't even read one another's faces. Their sex has the single-mindedness and limitations of masturbation; it doesn't pretend to be about anything other than feeling good.

Though Banks gives us no explicit details, the combination of the darkness, the rose-colored outside light tinting the flesh, and two people hungry for each other without restraint, apology or pretense adds up to a surprisingly erotic scene. The reader knows enough about the setting and the mood so that when Billy tells us their sex was "very sexual, straightforwardly sexual," we are almost challenged to fill in our own private details, making the scene as erotic as our imagination allows it to be.

- The setting of an adulterous sex scene—everything from the lighting to the landscape—can be a powerful element in heightening the level of illicitness and intrigue. Because the lovers are not supposed to be where they are, the setting itself is forbidden, an accomplice in the rendezvous. It can give you almost as much energy and information to work with as another character.

There is an abundance of sexual detail in my short story "Feasting," in which a man and woman married to other people have an intense long-distance affair that is fueled by their flirtation with sex games they do not play in their marriages. Some of the dramatic tension that drives the story arises from the ongoing conflict between them over how far to take their fantasies. Because they talk about these matters on the telephone more often than they see each other, there is a quality of extended foreplay—and ongoing titillation—that would have been exhausted much sooner had the lovers not been separated. This passage is from early in the story:

It was during one of those late, lavish phone calls that we first exchanged fantasies. . . . He wanted, he said, for me to touch myself while we were making love. "It would be erotic for you to be solicitous with your body."

He has had other fantasies and fascinations and has relentlessly sought my permission to explore them in phone call after phone call, as if my willingness, halfway across the country, made any difference. He has wanted me to wear black, lacy underwear and to take it off of me in elaborate, ritualistic stages and make love to me wearing only a black garter belt. It entered early and oddly into our conversation. One of the first nights we were together, I said, "I'll miss you tomorrow."

"Do you have any black underwear?"

"What?"

"Do you have any black underwear?"

"I just said I'll miss you and you said do you have any black underwear. Did I miss something?"

"No. Do you?"

"No. Just pastels."

This is the first dialogue between the characters, and it establishes the conflicts that will propel them through the story: the tension between affection and sex, between their needs for emotional intimacy and for the "straightforwardly sexual." Because their time together is so limited and has such distinct boundaries, it's almost as if they must choose which course to take, how best to use their time. Here, as elsewhere in the story, he wants to steer things toward experimentation that his marriage does not have room for, and she wants to make an emotional connection—though she too, in a more tentative way, is keen to take sexual risks:

He has never said and I have never asked whether he asks his wife to wear black underwear as well. My husband has never mentioned black underwear or anything remotely like it to me. My husband is tender and dependable and ordinary in his lovemaking—except on rare occasions when he has had too many martinis—and I would be surprised if he wanted anything more of his lovers.

When I think of it, though, I remember that it was I who

made the first mention of unusual sexual interests to Patrick. And now I am sure that his wife does not wear black underwear to bed with him or indulge him in another taste we danced around and talked around for months. I told him, the first night we were together, that one of my lovers had spanked me, that it had been his idea. Patrick said he had never done that and wanted to know what it was like.

On the most obvious level, the conflict that gets played out is his eagerness to experiment versus her reluctance. Giving it an added frisson are the standard limitations of adultery: time, geography and emotional commitment. The characters surprise each other and the reader with revelations about sexual appetites that they reveal a little at a time, doing a very slow, long-distance striptease. They don't tell all in their first encounter. The story is, in part, an ode to adulterous sex, because it allows for experimentation and fantasy and gives the lovers a second chance to embark on an adult relationship whose limitations are generally accepted.

"Feasting" is an example of a piece of fiction in which the sex scenes are integral to the narrative, because they are integral to the relationship between the man and woman. As in many adulterous liaisons, characters meet only to have sex; the sex is not something they fit into the rest of their relationship. Sexual tension becomes the primary force of the narrative.

LAST WORDS ABOUT ADULTERY

Adultery can be a source of high drama and upheaval, or of quiet, anguished intrigue, an unlighted stick of dynamite that never brings the house down but that threatens to time and time again. For a writer, a sexual triangle founded on deception is blessed with its own inherent dramas: Will the lovers' secret life be revealed? Will the marriage or the love affair win out? Will the betrayed spouse find out and forgive? Will the jilted mistress retreat with dignity or boil up her lover's child's pet rabbit for dinner, as Glenn Close's character does in *Fatal Attraction*?

Whether your cheating-hearted characters get caught *in flagrante* or nearly implode in their efforts not to, be sure that the action of your story is driven by who your characters are and what they want, rather than by the outward dramas, or potential dramas, of adultery.

CHAPTER EIGHT

Sex, Please, but Hold the History and the Guilt

Recreational Sex

"He was not exactly as handsome as he had been the night before—no man ever is—but he was still pretty superb, and he was ready."

—Christopher Coe, *Such Times*

In other chapters of this book, we've looked at sexual encounters through the prism of the relationships of the people who have them: virgins; spouses; adulterers. The beneficiaries of "recreational sex" are—pick your terminology—dating, sleeping around, getting acquainted, falling in love, hooking up, picking up, or engaging in what Milan Kundera calls "erotic friendships" and what more prosaic friends and I used to call "friendship with sex." They are not betraying a spouse, a cause, or an internal or external set of moral strictures with their passion. They are looking for intimacy, closeness, love and a good time, which may last five minutes or long enough to make plans to bring the new item home for Christmas. This is sex without history, without guilt and, to shifting degrees, without commitment. Before the sexual revolution this species of pleasure was available only to men, artists, bohemians and Europeans, with the exception, some say, of the British. ("Continental people have sex life," said Hungarian immigrant George Mikes in 1946 in his book *How to Be an Alien*, "the English have hot-water bottles.") Today, we are all eligible.

What does all this (mostly) unencumbered frolicking mean for fiction writers?

Writing about recreational sex is kind of like having it: The sex is the main event, and though it lacks the inherent drama of the illicit, it offers other possibilities for excitement and connection. Unlike married sex, it has no history and no certain future; it can lead anywhere or nowhere. The stakes are not inherently high, at least at the beginning, though they may become so faster than anyone intended. In his first novel, *An American Romance,* John Casey captures the paradoxical nature of casual sex, to some degree of all sexual encounters—that people can be physical intimates but emotional strangers—when his main characters, Anya and Mac, two graduate students at the University of Chicago, make love for the first time and drift off to sleep with Mac thinking: "He wished he knew her well enough to speak."

Without furtiveness, history or a future to focus on, the writer must use the encounter to some or all of these ends: to give us information about the characters; to give us a status report on the relationship, on the role and meaning of sex in it; and, through the dialogue, voice, interior monologue and details, to offer other insights into characters or into the narrator, as James Salter does with his voyeuristic narrator in *A Sport and a Pastime.*

The transformation from casual sex to deepening intimacy is articulated movingly in this passage from Joseph Olshan's *Nightswimmer,* set in gay New York in the 1990s:

> The first feast of another man's body is both joyful and confusing. I want to fill myself with everything, every nipple and biceps and every inch of cock, but I want to savor it and that demands more than one occasion. When I know a man for a while, when the parts of his body become familiar to me, as his own scent that I carry on my clothes, on my forearms, when he ceases to become just a name and becomes a familiar man, that's when the real sex begins. By then he's told me private things, and I know something of his story; and when I reach over to touch him in a bed that we've both slept in night after night, nothing casual, no matter how galvanic, can rival the power of that touch. For that touch is now encoded with the knowledge that I could lose everything, and

movement by movement, as I make love, I'm more completely aware of what I stand to lose.

One of the most talked about recent examples of sexually explicit writing is Harold Brodkey's short story "Innocence," first published in 1973 (a good year for recreational sex). It is the story of two seniors at Harvard, the narrator, Wiley, who falls in love with a beautiful woman, Orra ("To see her in sunlight was to see Marxism die"), who, though she has had lovers for six years, has never had an orgasm. If casual sex often leaves writers with a lack of conflict for their characters to act out, "Innocence" is shot through with dramatic tension: Almost every time they make love, Wiley is determined to make her come and she is determined to resist. For twenty densely written pages, they battle it out between the sheets (he wins, of course). Brodkey captures for us every physical and psychic flutter that passes between them. It's too long and too tightly written to be excerpted here. It appears in his collection, *Stories in an Almost Classical Mode*.

GIVEN CIRCUMSTANCES

1. Unless they are the friends who fall into bed together, the characters probably don't know each other well.
2. They have few if any commitments to one another or to anyone else.
3. They have individual sexual histories but not a common one.
4. They may have other sex partners currently in circulation.
5. They may be sexually uninhibited but emotionally guarded.
6. They may have vastly different expectations of the encounter.

EXAMPLES

An awareness of divergent expectations plagues the plucky narrator of Pam Houston's story, "How to Talk to a Hunter," in which a single woman is drawn again and again to a man who is trouble and who ropes her in with sex and a rugged exoticism. Writing in the second person, she is full of self-mockery and self-effacement over this Great Western outdoorsman who, on their first night at his place, asks if she wants to sleep under "skins or blankets." She tells us: "You will spend every night in this man's bed without asking yourself why he listens to top-forty country. Why he donated money to the Republican

Party. Why he won't play back his messages while you are in the room." Why can't she give him up? "The sun on the windows will lure you out of bed, but he'll pull you back under. The next two hours he'll devote to your body. With his hands, with his tongue, he'll express what will seem to you like the most eternal of loves. . . . Even in bed; especially in bed, you and he cannot speak the same language."

Her best friends tell her the hunter is bad news; he has other girlfriends; he's evasive; when she tells him she loves him, he answers, "I feel exactly the same way." But she cannot resist:

> Play Willie Nelson's "Pretty Paper." He'll ask you to dance, and before you can answer he'll be spinning you around your wood stove, he'll be humming in your ear. Before the song ends he'll be taking off your clothes, setting you lightly under the [Christmas] tree, hovering above you with tinsel in his hair. Through the spread of the branches the all-white lights you insisted on will shudder and blur, outlining the orna-ments he brought: a pheasant, a snow goose, a deer.

These teasing but virtually chaste sexual encounters fit perfectly with the narrator's guardedness, the hurt she is trying to rewrite in the face of the hunter's continuing rejection. She feels vulnerable, afraid of expressing her feelings because she knows they will not be returned and so is doing what she can to control the situation: keeping up a snappy patter, constructing a polished surface to hide the emotional turmoil underneath, letting us know she knows she is being mistreated—and that she has what it takes to handle it with panache. It would have been out of character for her to reveal too much more of herself in a graphic sex scene, given how much she has already exposed of her unreciprocated and ill-advised longings.

- Recreational sex often begins with both partners feeling care-free and uncommitted, which is not a good omen for creating dramatic conflict. Conflict develops when one character's feelings move at a different pace, and in a different direction, from the other's, as happens quickly in this story.
- You can keep conflict going, as Pam Houston does here, by involving characters outside the relationship, as when the woman consults her friends for advice.

• There is nothing more important in revealing who characters are than specific details in dialogue and description.

The narrator of Jane DeLynn's very smart and sassy novel *Don Juan in the Village* is always on the prowl, looking for love, sex and adventure in places where "women like me"—lesbians—are welcome: Key West, Ibiza, Italy, L.A., bars in downtown New York. The variety of sexual episodes is vast, and the narrator is self-effacing, ironic and wonderfully observant. She enjoys her escapades as much for the cheap thrills and outside possibility they may lead to love as for the stories they will give her to tell years later. In my interview with her, DeLynn observed that what is erotic is "obviously in the realm of the mind." The workings of her narrator's mind play a key role in her sex scenes.

On a trip to Italy in the early 1970s, where the narrator has gone to recuperate from a deep depression set off by her apartment burning down, she encounters a wealthy, older Italian man with a "young and beautiful" girlfriend "who did not confine her sexual interests exclusively to persons of one gender." Their three-way rendezvous takes place in the woman's apartment, where Carlo and Francesca proceed to undress the narrator and turn her slowly around:

> I found this impersonal inspection of my body extremely arousing. The American women I had slept with were either lesbians who were still embarrassed by their attraction to women or feminists who pretended that the reason they slept with women was not sexual but ideological; this casual acceptance of the carnality of our transaction seemed to me the essence of European sophistication.

A few minutes later. Carlo and Francesca

> seemed fascinated by my great wetness. I explained to them I had had *una problema* and had been unable to make love for a long time and now that I could it was very exciting. The word "*problema*" seemed to upset Francesca and I tried to explain that the kind of problem I meant was of the head rather than the body, that my apartment had burned down and I had become sick—that is, tired—of the life. They looked at me uncomprehendingly. . . .
>
> I felt happier and more comfortable than I had in ages— partially on account of the revival of my sexual desire, but

even more, I think because of the exoticness of the situation.
I imagined both the story I would tell my friends and the one
I would write about this . . . [and] I liked not understanding
what was being said. . . .

After Carlo and Francesca have intercourse, she observes that
Francesca was more excited by Carlo than by herself:

> I realized, with the slight surprise that always accompanies
> such revelations, that there really were women who liked men
> better than women—better even than a woman as remarkable
> as myself. It occurred to me I might have been brought there
> less for Francesca's sake than for Carlo's.

These passages are wonderful examples of the two-things-
happening-at-once principle: On the surface, they tell the story of a
casual ménage à trois between virtual strangers. Had DeLynn stuck
to describing the three-way mechanics, the scene could have read
like instructions for assembling a jungle gym. But the narrator's comments and observations fill out the encounter and add these elements: conflicts between characters and between cultures; revelations
about the narrator's feelings and vulnerabilities that probably were
not apparent to Carlo and Francesca; a historic dimension that lo-
cates us at a time in history, the early 1970s, when the collision of the
women's movement and the lesbian rights movement made sexual
encounters between women politically loaded in the ways that
DeLynn's narrator describes.

The sexual ambience in British writer Alan Hollinghurst's novel
The Swimming Pool Library is intense, compulsive and not at all re-
strained, except in the writing, which provides a chilling counterpoint
to the characters' sexual abandon. It tells of the sexual peregrinations
of William Beckwith, a young, directionless, gay aristocrat during the
summer of 1983, "the last summer of its kind there was ever to
be—" before AIDS made its mark on sex habits in England. Though
the novel seems at first loosely plotted, driven almost entirely by the
sexual urges of Beckwith and his far-ranging, biracial set (gay men
from sixteen to eighty-three), a more complex architecture emerges,
and the story extends its ambitions dramatically, putting each sexual
encounter into the context of England's treatment of gay men

throughout the twentieth century, using their plight as a symbol of state-sponsored and condoned bigotry.

In my letter to Hollinghurst, I asked this question: "AIDS hovers over the narrative. Did its lurking presence make you feel any sense of defiance or abandon in writing the sex scenes?" Here is his answer:

> I planned the book in the earliest 80s, and even when I started writing it at the beginning of 1984, AIDS, though already a major thing in the US, had hardly begun to be comprehended in Britain. . . . Then, in November 1984, a close friend of mine in London died of it; and over the following months I had to make a decision as to whether or not to incorporate into the novel a recognition of this disease which was so grimly altering the very world that much of the book was about. In the end, as you know, I decided to set it firmly in the hot summer in 1983; but of course the book took on a newly historic character that I could not have foreseen when I first imagined it. And yes, the outburst of anti-gay hostility that followed the arrival of AIDS did make me all the keener to write about gay sex in an unapologetic way.

The Swimming Pool Library is such a brilliantly integrated novel, I hesitate to pull out a scene or two for demonstration purposes. Though each sex scene is superbly well written, the cumulative effect of them has even greater power. Beckwith shuttles between encounters with live-in or steady lovers and with strangers in movie theaters and clubs. According to an entry in his best friend's diary, he always picks men who are "vastly poor, & dimmer than himself—younger too. I don't think he's ever made it with anyone with a degree. It's forever these raids on the inarticulate." One such raid is on Arthur Hope, an unschooled seventeen-year-old black who, after a week of passion with Beckwith, is now hiding out in Beckwith's apartment after killing someone. Beckwith is torn between wanting to protect him, love him, and wanting to throw him out in order to reclaim his apartment and his privacy:

> We barely used language at all to communicate: he sulked and thought I was putting him down if I made complicated remarks, and sometimes I felt numb at the compromise and self-suppression I submitted to. . . . But then in sex he lost his awkwardness.

On another occasion not long after, Beckwith is again fed up with the burden of Arthur's presence and the disturbing power of his attraction to Arthur:

> My whole wish was to throw things around, make a storm to dispel the stagnant heat, assert myself. Yet I found myself fastidiously tidying up, tight-lipped, not looking at him. He followed me helplessly around. . . . He was confused, wanted to be ready to do what I wanted, but found he could only annoy me further. Then I hurled the stack of newspapers I was collecting across the floor and went for him—pulled the trousers down over his narrow hips without undoing them, somehow tackled him onto the carpet, and after a few seconds' brutal fumbling fucked him cruelly. He let out little compacted shouts of pain, but I snarled at him to shut up and with fine submission he bit them back.
>
> Afterwards I left him groaning on the floor and went into the bathroom. I remember looking at myself, pink, excited, horrified, in the mirror.

A few minutes later, Beckwith goes back to Arthur, cradles him, and tells him how much he loves him. He then tells us that

> There were several occasions of this kind, when I was exposed by my own mindless randiness and sentimentality . . . our affair had started as a crazy fling with all the beauty for me of his youngness and blackness. . . . I saw him becoming more and more my slave and my toy, in a barely conscious abasement which excited me even as it pulled me down.

This scene is convincing and compelling for many reasons. The writing is vivid, precise, and full of unflinching, unflattering candor and insight about the narrator and Arthur, whose very lack of speech is a large part of his character, and one of his appeals to Beckwith.

The sexual encounter—actually more of an attack—occurs in the context of the entire, unequal relationship, and mirrors the relationship with an accuracy troubling to Beckwith. He has every social advantage over Arthur; sexual domination is the final hold he can have over him, and he exerts it. Sex for Beckwith is as much an assertion of power and class as it is a grab for pleasure. The irony is that even Beckwith's pedigree as a member of the aristocracy does not protect him from the prejudice and violence he suffers elsewhere in the novel because he is gay.

At the heart of this and other sex scenes is Hollinghurst's exploration of the complexities and contradictions in our urges for sex, intimacy and connection.

The direct, matter-of-fact language of the sexual encounter matches the nature of the sex as well as the narrator's blunt, almost confessional attitude toward his actions.

- In your own sex scenes involving characters whose connection is primarily sexual, who have no particular responsibilities to one another and do not know each other well, a narrator or main character who keeps trying to understand his partner or understand the nature of his attraction to his partner, as Hollinghurst does here, can add tension, complexity and insight to a relatively hollow encounter.

The last gasps of the AIDS-free sexual revolution—from a very different vantage point—were also at the center of my first novel, *Slow Dancing*, set around the election of Ronald Reagan in 1980. I conceived of the story as being about two sexually liberated thirty-year-old women, best friends who wanted to go "on the record" with their lives. In other words, abandon the emotionally empty, often furtive, casual sexual relationships they had craved during their twenties and trade them in for something more stable and less secretive, hence "on the record." The novel came to be about the failure of sex to give my characters the emotional connections they came slowly to admit that they wanted. I was also keen to explore the sleight of hand that is in the nature of lovemaking: the promise, constantly dashed, that the intimacy of the moment will last beyond the finish line.

The book opens with Lexi, a lawyer for the poor, on her way to dinner with the man with whom she will eventually go "on the record." Driving to dinner, she remembers her early days as a lawyer—and lover to Stephen Shipler, an older, slick lawyer, a distant, icy man to whose chilly charms she was oddly susceptible. During the first sex Lexi has with him she is completely focused on the mechanics; she is so out of touch with her emotions that it is not until the next morning when he leaves her that she allows herself to feel anything. Even then she is more comfortable sizing up Shipler to see what she can learn from him than admitting she might have feelings for him. The first night:

> In his hotel room he used his hands to hold her head, moved it with deliberate but tempered force—far more than a suggestion—from a spot on his neck to his chest to himself. He kept his hands pressed firmly to her ears, then played with strands of her hair. He moved her head then away from himself so that he could feel her breasts there, between her breasts, and he pressed them close around it, which no one had ever. . . . It was weird having it pushed into her face, pushed against her, as casually as if it were a finger. He was so sure of himself. So cock-centered. The phrase had never occurred to her before that moment, when it was locked between her breasts.
>
> When he was inside of her later, she felt the same taut, sure strength in his hips as they pressed into her, forcing her to press back. . . . With his hips he pulled her along to the edge of sensation and then let her pull back ever so gently, and back and forth and back and forth. She felt as if she were getting ready for a dive, jumping up and down on the end of the diving board to get a feel for the springs. Tighter than she had expected. Though she offered no resistance and came right before he did.
>
> When they caught their breath and pulled the covers back up, Stephen kissed her on the cheek, a quick goodnight kiss, and rolled over and slept by himself.

The next morning, she pretends to sleep while he packs; they say goodbye blandly and he departs:

> Lexi turned over, drew the cover up around her and thought: How many women has he left like this in hotel rooms? A bit surprised by the cheap drama of the thought, and how it had come to her full-blown, like a jingle from a commercial or the refrain of a song, mass-produced and ready for consumption by the broken-hearted. She was a little broken-hearted, but she was also intrigued by the constellation of circumstances: his law-firm smooth, his odious charm, his cock. The wallflower gets laid by the captain of the football

team and even though she knows it's not love—and it may not even be romance—it's its own sort of triumph. Even if you have to keep it a secret. . . .

. . . there were some things she wanted to learn from Stephen Shipler. One of them was that captain-of-the-football-team confidence . . . [though] Stephen Shipler was not the kind of lawyer she wanted to be. He wasn't even the kind of man she would want to have around on a regular basis. One of the ones you see three times a week, introduce to your friends and spend a lot of time talking to about where your relationship is going. She knew where her relationship with Stephen Shipler was going. . . . He would teach her to be comfortable in fancy restaurants, . . . dress like a woman instead of a college student, and he would teach her something about fucking. Something about taking what you want when you want it, which seemed to be one of the things he did best.

Still, she was pleased that Stephen Shipler had taught her his coldness, and taught her some of the other things she had had in mind. It made it easier the next time.

In this scene, as in Alan Hollinghurst's, the casual sexual encounter is not dropped into the story and then abandoned, but woven tightly into the narrative so that *the encounter has an effect on the character*. In this case, it causes Lexi to change her behavior (take up with Stephen for her own chilly reasons) and perceive herself differently (as someone who can *choose* lovers for their practical, not sentimental, value). The encounter provokes a multiplicity of reactions and leads ultimately to the tough-talking attitude that Lexi professes in the novel's opening line.

The only choice I regret, reading over the scene more than a decade after I wrote it, is the "himself" (twice!) in the opening paragraph instead of "penis," "prick" or "cock." I don't remember what inspired this lapse into coyness in my otherwise unabashed narrative. It doesn't work because "himself" is not what Lexi thinks when she has her face shoved in his crotch, and it's not what Stephen Shipler would call his penis. "Himself," prudish and indirect as it is, would be a fine choice if it were the word the character used or thought when considering that part of the anatomy.

In her novel *Waiting to Exhale*, Terry McMillan deals deftly with the "himself" issue—as well as contraceptives and AIDS protection—without naming names. In an early scene between Robin, one of the four girlfriends who narrates the novel, and her pudgy new suitor, Michael, McMillan captures the narrator's sassy blend of experience, curiosity, anticipated disappointment and blustery longing—while making the sexual stage directions an integral part of the narrative. Robin takes off her sweater and bra, Michael's eyes bulge with appreciation, and he slips under the covers with his boxer shorts still on,

> before I got a chance to see what he had to offer.
> "I knew you were going to be beautiful all over," he said, after I got under the covers. "And you smell so good." He put his little fat hand over one of my breasts and squeezed. My nipples immediately deflated.
> "Do you have protection, or should I get it?" I asked.
> "Right here," he said, pulling it from the side of the bed. He took his shorts off and threw them on the floor. Then he put his hands under the covers, and his shoulders started jerking, which meant he was having a rough time getting it on.
> "Do you need some help?" I asked.
> "No no no," he said. "There." He rolled over on top of me, and since I could no longer breathe, let alone move, I couldn't show him how to get me in the mood. He started that slurpy kissing again, and I felt something slide inside me. At first I thought it was his finger, but no, his hands were on the headboard. Then he sort of pushed, and I was waiting for him to push again, so he could get it all the way in, but when he started moving, that's when I realized it was. I was getting pissed off about now, but I tried to keep up with his little short movements, and just when I was getting used to his rhythm he started moving faster and faster and he squeezed me tight against his breasts and yelled, "*God this is good!*" and then all of his weight dropped on me. Was he for real? I just kind of lay there, thinking: Shit, I could've had a V-8. . . .

This scene works in part because Robin comes to it with a very specific ambition: She is interviewing this guy for the position of lifelong companion, after a long history of unsatisfying relationships. She comes to it with both an expectation *and* an attitude: sassy skepticism. The conflict and comedy arise from the clashing of her huge ambition for the occasion, her jaundiced attitude, and poor Michael's merely human fumblings.

Sex is Robin's way to judge the worth of the man and the future of the relationship, certain that if he cannot satisfy her sexually, she cannot count on him to satisfy her emotionally. She is prepared to call it quits and cut her losses, but moments later, Michael surprises her by soliciting her feelings, asking what she wants from life, and expressing his fondness for her. When they make love again a short time later, she manages to forget that he's fat, short and pale. Instead of accentuating the comedy of the encounter, she allows herself to tumble to the unexpected emotional warmth of it.

- When your characters come to sexual encounters with different expectations, these differences lead to friction, conflict and, in some cases, comedy. All you need to know as you begin to write a sex scene is what *one* character's expectations are. Conflict sets in when the other character can't or won't give her what she wants.

Max and Nora, the lovers in Glenn Savan's novel *White Palace*, are an unlikely pair, well suited, it seems, only in the sack, where their differences set off enough sparks to send the Space Shuttle into orbit. He's a bookish, ambitious twenty-seven-year-old Jewish widower; she's a forty-one-year-old, tough-talking, hard-drinking, Reagan-loving White Palace waitress. Nora has any number of secrets from Max, the darkest about her son Charley, who she told Max had died of leukemia. When Nora's sister Judy visits—the first time they have seen each other since Charley's funeral—Judy reveals the truth to Max, that Charley died at fourteen of a drug overdose, horribly neglected by both parents. Max does not mention this revelation to Nora. This scene takes place that night, with Max and Nora sleeping in the living room and the visitors in the bedroom. (We've learned before that Nora has gynecological problems and cannot conceive any longer.)

Nora entered the living room naked, a bad idea with guests in the house, and from the weave of her walk he could see how drunk she was. She got into bed beside him and turned unceremoniously upon her back. Max wasn't sure if this contained a sexual invitation or not. Such complete passivity on her part was unknown to him—except for those times when he started things rolling by applying his mouth to her. This he began to do, swiftly losing himself in the flowery complexities of her labia, until her thighs tightened in refusal and she sat up, taking his face between her hands. "Just fuck me," she said.

She lay back down and waited.

"Right now?"

"Yes."

She waited stoically, like a good Victorian wife. She felt abnormally tight as he entered her. And then there was a further surprise; she was silent. He thought this might be in deference to Bob and Judy down the hall, but that didn't explain what her eyes were doing open, or why the look in them was so liquid and beseeching.

"Max," she said, just as he was starting to come apart against his climax. "Max, I have to tell you . . ."

"What?" he managed to say.

"I just wish . . ."

"What?"

"I just wish we could have a baby."

For an irrational moment he wished it, too. And then he spurted his useless seed.

The details of their sex life are well documented in the novel, so that when we come to this scene, several months into the stormy affair, we know how different it is from earlier encounters; Max takes note of all differences and wonders what accounts for them, which creates a bit of dramatic tension. Though told from Max's point of view, by the end of the scene, we can well imagine what has been going through Nora's head since her sister's arrival that she has not shared with Max: a replay of her son's death and the troubled life that led to it. The author uses the scene to reveal the ongoing anguish that Nora feels but cannot express except when lovemaking lowers her defenses. The scene also shows us—and Max—that Nora feels much more than a sexual connection with him, while Max can only allow himself a momentary fantasy of that kind of commitment to her.

- You can make a sex scene a turning point in your story when your characters do or say something especially revealing while making love.

The highly erotic and finely chiseled sex scenes in James Salter's novel *A Sport and a Pastime* fall technically in the category of "recreational sex" but could as easily find a place under "voyeurism" and "fantasies." Doing triple duty in this way gives the scenes an emotional richness and an intense sexual charge that draw one back to the novel again and again.

Set in France in the early 1960s, it tells the story of a pair of young lovers, a twenty-four-year-old Yale graduate named Dean who takes up with a young French shop girl, Anne-Marie. Occasionally Dean reports on the affair to a male friend, another young American, our narrator, who is traveling through France, studying its history and architecture, and imagining and re-creating for us the details of Dean and Anne-Marie's affair. Infrequently the narrator reminds us that this is *his* script, not the transcript of Dean and Anne-Marie: "I am not telling the truth about Dean, I am inventing him. I am creating him out of my own inadequacies, you must always remember that." But of course, we often forget it, as the author means us to, because the love scenes are so staggeringly real, which keeps adding to our sense of the narrator's loneliness. He has nothing to do but wallow in fantasies of someone *else's* affair. These fantasies, of course, are *his*, projected onto Dean—the safest sort of fantasies to have.

For example, in the scene that occurs before the one quoted below, Dean has talked to Anne-Marie about all "the ways to love, the sweet variety." When she asks what they are, Dean cannot say, though eventually we, and Anne-Marie, are meant to understand that the one he is most curious about is anal sex. Toward the end of the scene below, the mention of lubricants—and "frightening" evidence—refers to this:

> She is in a good mood. She is very playful. As they enter her building she becomes the secretary. They are going to dictate some letters. Oh, yes? She lives alone, she admits, turning on the stairs. Is that so, the boss says. *Oui.* In the room they undress independently. . . .

"Ah," she murmurs.

"What?"

"It's a big *machine à écrire.*"

She is so wet by the time he has the pillows under her gleaming stomach that he goes right into her in one long, delicious move. They begin slowly. When he is close to coming he pulls his prick out and lets it cool. Then he starts again, guiding it with one hand, feeding it in like line. She begins to roll her hips, to cry out. It's like ministering to a lunatic. Finally he takes it out again. As he waits, tranquil, deliberate, his eye keeps falling on lubricants—her face cream, bottles in the *armoire.* They distract him. Their presence seems frightening, like evidence. They begin once more and this time do not stop until she cries out and he feels himself come in long, trembling runs, the head of his prick touching bone, it seems. They lie exhausted, side by side, as if just having beached a great boat.

"It was the best ever," she says finally. "The best. . . . We must type more letters. . . ."

Were this scene a faithful account of the goings on of Dean and Anne-Marie, it would be a hugely impressive—and juicy—piece of writing. But it would lack the haunting, melancholy, self-punishing quality it has as the narrator's fantasy.

Reread the scene and take note of these elements:

• This is a fantasy within a fantasy; the narrator is imagining Dean and Anne-Marie acting out a fantasy (his own).

• There are very few adjectives or adverbs throughout.

• The scene is not dropped into the narrative but made to connect with what comes before, notably Dean's interest (read: the narrator's interest) in anal sex, which he wants but is ashamed to pursue.

• The writing, in part, has a pornographic intention and intensity: Its primary purpose is to arouse the narrator. Its secondary purpose is to make us understand—indeed, *feel physically*—the intensity of his longing, loneliness and shame.

It's easy to see that voyeurism and fantasy can be powerful elements in your characters' sexual encounters, but they are far more interesting if you can connect them to thematic and narrative issues in your work. In *A Sport and a Pastime*, a lonely narrator becomes a voyeur and fantasist, creating narratives so immediate that we forget he has invented them, just as the author of the book has invented *his* stories. Might we all be voyeurs?

LAST WORDS ABOUT RECREATIONAL SEX

There is nothing sweeter than the freedom to have sex without guilt or remorse, whether it is with your spouse of thirty years or a ragingly handsome new lover. As a fiction writer, that freedom means you will have to work awfully hard to create compelling sex scenes. Without internal or external dramas to stoke the engines that fuel essential conflicts and dramas, you really have to know your characters thoroughly, create clear distinctions between them, and exploit those differences with all the creative tools in your arsenal: your imagination, sense of drama, ability to empathize with your characters—and your determination to rewrite until you get it right.

CHAPTER NINE

Sex Forbidden by Law, History and Politics

The Illicit

"Adam was but human—this explains it all. He did not want the apple for the apple's sake; he wanted it because it was forbidden."

—Mark Twain, *Pudd'nhead Wilson*

S tepping out on a spouse isn't our only chance to sample the fruits of forbidden sex. In fact, adultery is pretty tame next to the sparks that can fly when characters violate laws and taboos beyond their marriage vows. We'll see what happens when Humbert Humbert moves in with a lonely widow so he can indulge his passion for her twelve-year-old daughter Lolita; when Auschwitz survivor Leon Solomon remembers his incestuous encounter with his sister, in Jerome Badanes' novel, *The Final Opus of Leon Solomon*; and when an American diplomat stationed in Leningrad during the Cold War has a dicey fling with a young Russian woman in my novel *Safe Conduct*. But there needn't be a war on to heat up the sheets; a Presidential election will do. The real-life romance between Democratic strategist James Carville and Republican spin doctor Mary Matalin during the 1992 election had some of us dying for a peek through the keyhole when these two fire-breathing rivals managed a few minutes to themselves.

Love that takes hold and thrives in a hostile environment is a rich, complex source of material for a writer, full of built-in sexual tension and possibilities for political, legal and psychic repercussions.

Forbidden sex can fuel a plot, give your characters a secret life to lead, define the atmosphere of a novel—of an entire historical period—and bring police, secret and otherwise, into the boudoir, if only via tape recorder and camera. Beyond the immediate advantages for the writer of working with characters who flaunt laws and conventions, on occasion a particularly hearty character becomes a symbol of resistance or liberation to readers who are similarly oppressed.

When England was a brutally hostile environment for homosexuality—celebrated playwright Oscar Wilde was jailed for two years in 1897 for homosexual activity; working-class men were routinely hanged in the nineteenth century—all a fictional character had to do was spend the night with someone of the same sex to become a hero or role model to generations of gays and lesbians. In *The Well of Loneliness* British author Radclyffe Hall's description of her heroine's first lesbian sexual encounter is limited to these few prim words: "and that night they were not divided," but they were enough. Soon after publication in 1928 the novel was banned (until 1948). E.M. Forster, by then well known for *A Room with a View* and *Howards End*, published twenty years earlier, campaigned against the banning. His own fiction involving homosexual characters, including the novel *Maurice*, was not published until after his death in 1971 and was greeted even then by American writers and critics with condescension and not such thinly veiled homophobia.

Times change and so do hostile environments. Nathaniel Hawthorne's Hester Prynne would not have to wear her scarlet *A* today. Copies of *Ulysses* are no longer seized by U.S. Customs agents. And British playwright Joe Orton's scandalously risqué dialogues of the mid-1960s are as inoffensive as La Rochefoucauld's aphorisms compared to the daily fare served up on afternoon TV with Geraldo, Sally Jesse and Ricki Lake. Apartheid is officially over and so is the Cold War, but for a writer with a nose for strange fruit, there are still stories to tell about sex that is forbidden by law, by convention or by history.

GIVEN CIRCUMSTANCES

Many of the same given circumstances of adulterous sex apply here as well, minus, of course, the betrayed spouse and the web of complications accompanying that deception.

1. The sex is preheated, charged by its illicit nature.
2. Lovers typically meet in secret; there's danger in being seen together and often a time limit on the meeting.
3. Because of the danger, lovers are often in a heightened state of awareness.
4. Characters who indulge in forbidden sex have secret lives.
5. Like adulterers, they may try to conceal evidence of their liaisons, not from a spouse but a parent, sibling, co-worker, authority figure—anyone who might take offense at, or take action against, their behavior.
6. Guilt may accompany feelings of exhilaration, liberation, rebelliousness, or, particularly in the case of gays and lesbians in a hostile environment, relief at no longer having to conceal their secret selves.
7. Context is everything. The writer must paint a vivid picture of the society or culture that forbids the sex to dramatize how much is at stake for the characters who violate its laws and conventions.
8. Sex scenes between illicit lovers often include references to the outside forces that attempt to keep the lovers apart.

EXAMPLES

There's more relief than satisfying sex when two lonely gay men arrange to meet in a beach-side changing shed in "Contact," a short story by Australian writer John Lonie. After communicating anonymously for several days via bathroom graffiti—"the tribal calling card"—the story's forty-year-old narrator slinks to the bushes with the young man whose handwriting he saw on the bathstall wall. Both are vacationing with their respective families (parents, grown siblings), far from the comforts of gay-friendly Australian cities. The narrator, who spends most of the holiday minding his young nieces and nephews—in a role he calls "the modern version of the family aunt"—pegs his cruel four-year-old nephew Hans a "poofter-basher [gay basher] in training." Out of loneliness, horniness, and feelings of separation from his "tribe" in the city, he takes a gamble on the anonymous invitation. But instead of the bathstall veteran he expects, a nervous seventeen-year-old, who looks even younger, shows up, bringing an intense, bittersweet reminder of the culture's "poofter-bashing" laws and attitudes.

The story concludes with their meeting, which the narrator intends to flee once he sees how young the young man is:

> I am about to say you're too young for me and I'm too old for you when I feel him trembling under my touch and he puts his hand up to my hand and presses it against his cheek. My heart melts. He's scared, so scared he's shaking, and I realize that it is he who's taken the huge risk, not me. I fold him in to me and hold him and he hangs on tightly, so tightly.
>
> His erection hasn't gone away and then he shudders and grabs me hard as I feel him come against my thigh. I hold him tight and press my face to his, stroking the back of his neck and head. Then I feel dampness on my cheek and he's crying softly. It's okay, I say quietly, hoping he feels safe with me, cry all you want. And he does.
>
> For ages, we stand there, him hanging on tight. I can hear his heart beat and the sound of the blood coursing through his veins, this stranger. I should be looking after him, not that little thug Hans or any of my nieces and nephews. They've got their parents. This one, he's my tribe, that's for sure. Who looks after him? Who looks after any of us at that time?
>
> . . . I tell him how brave he is, taking such a chance. So are you, he says, we're illegal up here, you know. Not "it's" illegal but "we're" illegal. He is so lonely, so very lonely, you can taste the need on his skin.
>
> Multiply him by thousands and what other way is there than the change rooms or a public toilet whose doors become a samizdat? And when as strangers we collide in that fleeting moment, the immensity of feeling between us creates such a closeness that we go on searching for it, desperate just once more to taste the sweetness it brings. It surely is the kindness of strangers.

This narrator follows his urge for an anonymous fling and ends up with far more than he expected—ends up, in the way of all good fiction, being surprised by the distance between what he wants and what he gets. The desire for anonymous sex is selfish and simple, but the pursuit of it—even a pursuit as single-minded as this one—forces unpredictable elements into the mix: the needs and frailties of other human beings. Had the narrator gotten exactly what he set out for, a beach-side bacchanal, there would have been no surprise, for him *or* for us. And not much of a story to tell.

In a scene about illicit sex, one or both characters may feel more fear than sexual excitement—fear of admitting what they are doing, fear that they will be caught, exposed and punished. As you reread this scene, pinpoint places where one character expresses fear and the other acknowledges it. The author goes on to use that emotion to propel the scene forward and convey the legal and political climate that causes the fear.

- The more fearful character is comforted by the narrator, whose own apprehensions have been overshadowed by the boy's.
- The narrator acquires a soothing strength in relation to the boy, instead of feeling, as he did at first, like a sexual predator.
- The boy's fear leads the narrator to reflect on his place in his family and culture and to realize where he must direct his allegiance.
- The last paragraph moves from the personal to the political with the narrator's comparison of the writings on bathroom doors to samizdat, highlighting the risk men are taking as well as the cause of free expression they assert in these messages.

The Cold War made sleeping with the enemy something of an occupational hazard for generations of Western diplomats and military men stationed in Communist countries. Once the Wall came down, it wasn't only the authors of Cold War thrillers who had to find new enemies for their heroes to slay; sex across international borders lost some of its dangerous edge.

In the days when it was still razor sharp, the male lead in my novel *Safe Conduct*, diplomat Eli ("Mac") MacKenzie, got involved with a young Russian woman, Lida, while working in the U.S. consulate on assignment to Leningrad in 1974. Though married at the time, he and his wife, who remained in the U.S., had an open marriage in which they even told one another about their love lives. Once he returned to the U.S., Mac and Lida were both punished by their governments for the affair and forced to stop communicating. Seventeen years later, after the Berlin Wall came down, Lida, now living in the West, calls Mac and they arrange to meet. The catch is that Mac is now married to a new wife, Kate Lurie, who knows the story of Mac and Lida. She accompanies him to the reunion, and as narrator of the novel, she remembers and reimagines the story Mac told her years before, at a time when Lida's reappearance in his life was as remote as the collapse of the Soviet Empire.

Using Kate to narrate these events gives the story and the sex scenes a multiplicity of dimensions. The sex scenes can be about far more than what goes on or went on between the lovers.

Here's part of Kate's re-creation of Mac and Lida's first night together in bed in his Leningrad apartment. (Earlier Mac told Lida that his apartment is bugged; Lida told him that "the Komitet" is Soviet slang for the KGB.)

> "And your wife—are you sure she'll be happy you're in bed with me?"
>
> "Lida, I don't want you to think that this might turn into something else, I—"
>
> "Come on, I'm kidding. Don't be so serious all the time."
>
> "But I am serious." He did not mean to sound stern. He ran his hand down the length of her voluptuous torso. "Serious about this."
>
> "You are, aren't you." It was not a question. She stretched her back against the bed. "Very serious."
>
> "And this."
>
> She nodded, made a faint sound that came from the back of her throat. Her back arced, her legs fell open. When he looked up at her face, eyes shut, cheek hard against the pillow, he noticed a small scar. For a few seconds it distracted him. Then her hips began to rock, and he was surprised to hear her speak. "Let's give them something to remember."
>
> "Who?"
>
> "The Komitet. And everyone else who's listening."

Later in the novel, while at Mac's apartment, Lida calls a friend from high school who works for the KGB, just to be sure she can get in touch with him, in case she needs protection: She is taking a risk sleeping with a U.S. diplomat who is automatically considered a spy by the KGB. After the phone call she asks Mac what she should do if the KGB contacts her and asks about her relationship with him. "You can tell them anything I've told you," he answers. They are about to leave for a bar; she is going to borrow a shirt of his. Again, this is Mac's point of view as reported and re-created by his new wife Kate:

> The rules here are meant only to keep you off balance, keep you guessing about where the real danger lies. It's everywhere, isn't it? That's what they want you to think. Maybe it's true. But whoever is listening on the headphones, labeling and cataloging the reels of tape—this is the only conclusion they will be able to reach: Lida and Mac are practically starved. She turns to ask about the shirt she will borrow and it is no more than the startling aquamarine of her eyes that draws him across the room. She undoes his pants with one hand and the buttons of her blouse with the other. What thrills him more than any specific sensation is the blunt fact of her desire. She wants this as much as he does. . . . She kneels and rubs her nipples against his knees, her tongue to the crease of his scrotum. He will tell [his wife] her name, that he met her in a restaurant, that her father is in the military, but how can he possibly tell her that beneath the eyes of the secret police, a love affair with every single sigh on tape—How can he tell his wife that in this country of vast, unspeakable sorrows, where the newsreels of his childhood, the Siege in the dead of winter, play around the clock, he is happier than he has been in years?

Though neither scene is especially graphic, both depict oral sex: cunnilingus, in the first example, fellatio, in the second. In both, the moments of sexual contact are very compressed and much less direct than they would have been if I had used slang or a more clinical description. Instead, in both cases, I have made the reader work a bit to figure out whose body parts are where. Also, instead of focusing on the progress of the sexual activity, on the orgasm, I focus on the characters' awareness of being watched by the KGB. I allow the characters to be turned on by this, but I also mean for the reader to remember, with a bit of a jolt, that it is Kate narrating and inventing the scenes. The reader might conclude (as I meant her to) that Kate feels both threatened and aroused by her inventions; and that she has taken the place of the KGB in her own paranoia and voyeurism.

I depicted the sexual contact so indirectly because I felt Kate would be so threatened by these moments she would not want to imagine them more explicitly.

- When writing about sex in a police state or under surveillance, the presence of other eyes and ears on the scene, and in the scene, can easily lead the characters toward fantasy and voyeurism.

In a situation where a government tries to use sex to blackmail its adversaries, you can get a lot of mileage out of weaving politics into sex scenes and sex into political scenes, as Julius Lester does in his novel based loosely on the life of Dr. Martin Luther King Jr., *And All Our Wounds Forgiven*. It's set in the present and told by four characters looking back on the turbulent 1960s, including the wife of slain civil rights leader John Calvin Marshall, his young blonde mistress, Elizabeth, and Marshall himself, speaking to us (in lowercase letters) from the great beyond but wise to all that's happened in the years since his assassination.

The night after leading a major civil rights march in Washington, DC, Marshall is summoned from the hotel room he's sharing with Elizabeth to the office of the FBI Director, a dead-ringer for J. Edgar Hoover. This political confrontation is essential to our understanding of the times, of Marshall's character and commitment, and the context for his intense sexual connection with Elizabeth. The FBI Director is the first to speak in Marshall's account of the event:

> "i listened to that speech of yours yesterday and it made me sick. . . ."
>
> he had a folder in front of him and shoved it across the desk at me.
>
> "what do you think the american people would say if they saw some of those pictures? i've got tapes, too. i'll say this for you: you can make the bedsprings squeak."
>
> i opened the folder to see a grainy photograph of a naked elizabeth astride the naked me. beneath it there were more: she with my penis in her mouth, me with my head between her legs, me atop her, me entering her anally.
>
> there was such a welter of emotions: embarrassment, shock and anger and outrage that i had no privacy any more. yet i was also fascinated. we all have photographs of ourselves at picnics, family reunions, weddings, graduations. but we never

have the chance to see ourselves making love. part of me
wanted elizabeth to see the photos and to reminisce with her
about where we had been in this photo and where in
that one.

behind the photos was a sheaf of papers, a log of the motels
and hotels in which we had made love. i knew we made love
a lot but seeing it documented that way, i couldn't help but
be impressed.

The director then tells Marshall that unless he withdraws from
political activism, he will send copies of these photographs to the
press and to Marshall's wife. Marshall's answer: "do you need any
help licking the stamps?"

This is a confrontation between good and evil, between a man of
unlimited power and no scruples and an underdog with a just cause.
The surprise here for Marshall is to find out that even while making
love, he cannot escape his public self; that his enemies are prepared
to use everything, including his sexual appetites, to extinguish his
commitment to justice. The surprise for the reader in this scene is
Marshall's unexpected delight in this package of explosive evidence
meant to be used against him.

This is not, of course, a sex scene, but a scene in which we see
a corrupt government trying to use sexual activity as a weapon of
control.

• In writing about people under surveillance or people subject
to blackmail, the blackmailers can become characters in your story,
whether or not they actually meet the people they are attempting
to control. But if they do meet, confrontations are a dramatic opportunity for victims to learn their private lives have been moni-
tored and confront their opponents face-to-face.

Sex and politics need not be played for such high stakes to create
disturbances in the field. In British writer Roger King's darkly erotic
novel *Sea Level*, the characters' attitudes toward sex are essential to
the story. Narrated by a malcontented economist, Bill Bender, whose
international consulting work takes him to troubled Third World
countries where he is supposed to improve living conditions for the
poor, he is estranged from his wife, a sexually repressed, upper-
class French woman, Mireille. When a colleague—a determined,

straight-talking Chinese woman named Han—asks if she can accompany him on trips to the Third World, as a way to gain the necessary experience so that she can be promoted from "statistical assistant" to "professional staff," he is ripe for the asking:

> She was intelligent, knew the work, went straight to the point. Unlike genteel Mireille, she was most at ease naked, her knees fallen apart; she liked it in the light, in dangerous places. She had an energy, a hunger; we were formidable. My father, I felt sure, would sense the wantonness in her, the absence of niceness, and be appalled. I liked that too, the break of it, the shedding of all that slavish fear, respect for betters, all that settling for half a loaf. She didn't ask me to be dutiful, didn't claim my obedience with hers; she only invited me to take her on. Or so it seemed to me.
>
> I had said in my office that night [when she asks if she can accompany him on trips], playing to her script, "And what will you do for me?" She had played it mock Chinese, pulling her schoolgirl glasses down her nose with a calculated winsomeness: "Suk yor kok?" She had me then. I was lost then.

Bender's comparisons of his wife to Han are as much an attempt to understand the women as to understand his own attraction to them, his dual desires to play it safe and to court danger. With Han on a trip to Liberia, where they are supposed to be improving the lives of the poor, he goes along with her brazen exhibitionism.

> I look, though Han does not, at the face of the old woman pressed against the window of our car. She is poor, one of the ones Han wished us to be among while we did this. The woman may be nearly blind, which could be why she's approached so close; I can't tell from the blankness of her eyes. Han is not looking at the woman but is twisted back to look at me. She wears only a blouse, which is undone. She's on my lap and I'm still high up inside her; her hand is still in place underneath herself. She ignores the old woman, a hand's length away, whose inexpressive eyes sweep back and forth over us. On our side of the glass the temperature is comfortable. On the old woman's side it is more than a hundred degrees. We are in Liberia. Han has twisted back to me, the

little wry smile on her face, somehow pleased. I look from the old woman with her flaps of empty breasts pressed up against the door—surely the metal is burning her flesh—to Han's wry smile. Though I can't hear her, she has just said, "That was weird!" in a tone of deep gratification. I am definitely with Han.

Bender tells us later that he felt excitement as well as disgust, "either at the act or the fool she made of me." Such is the power of sex, that it can drive us to commit acts that offend others, that put ourselves in danger, and that mock and belittle our avowed ambitions, in this case, to help the poor of Liberia.

• In order to make a character's exhibitionism believable, as Han's is, the author must have established traits beforehand that suggest behavior so antisocial might flow from them. Because Bender acquiesces, we must also know enough about him beforehand to find his actions credible.

The narrator of *The Final Opus of Leon Solomon* by Jerome Badanes is an Auschwitz survivor and a scholar of Jewish history who is about to commit suicide. In New York City in the 1980s, Leon Solomon is tormented by his past—his parents' early deaths, his sister's murder by the Nazis in the streets of Warsaw, his time in Auschwitz, his failed marriage—and certain of a bleak future after being caught stealing pages from Jewish documents in the 42nd Street Library and selling them to the Harvard Judaica Society: He will be barred forever from libraries. He checks into a hotel of faded splendor and on a stack of yellow legal pads, he composes his final opus: the story of his life.

The novel has surprised many readers in its sexually explicit scenes, almost all having to do with forbidden sex: the near-incest between Leon and his severely arthritic sister as they tried to pass for Aryans in Nazi-occupied Warsaw; sex the Nazis force on young Solomon and a prostitute as they watch; and the torrid, three-night affair between Solomon and his neighbor, Kirstin Dietrich, the daughter of a Gestapo officer, around the time he was stealing from the library.

During their hiding in Warsaw, Solomon came close to making love to his sickly younger sister; he regrets now that he didn't. "That restraint of mine was a crime against my doomed sister. I consider that lack of defiance against the Nazis, and against God, too, if you will, my gravest sin." His other crime against her was that he did not poison her before the Nazis beat her to death and left her in a public square, "to instill terror in any Poles still harboring Jews." In the world that Hitler made—and that Badanes re-creates in his novel— certain acts of incest and murder are a kind of grace. His sister had been a promising concert pianist crippled by arthritis.

> Every night after that I carefully soaped Malkele from her long graceful neck down to each and every toe. Though her limbs were atrophied and her spine bent slightly backwards, her small breasts remained girlish and as lovely as her face. Soaping Malkele, slowly, gently, quietly, became for us our kaddish for our obscured childhood and for our dead mother and father. This soaping was our only defense against the looming Nazi death machinery. During the day we longed for those few moments of slippery tenderness. My own muscles craved it as much as hers.
>
> Yes, yes, we were, after a fashion, Malkele and I, lovers. But we obeyed the final taboo—we never, to be cold and German about it, fornicated. I washed her hair. She still cursed and threatened me. I soaped every inch of her body. I caressed her pointy nipples with the palm of my hand. I dried her and helped her into her nightgown. I carried her to her bed. I brushed her thick reddish black hair in the candle-lit bedroom. Once she whispered to me, "To what are Chopin's Preludes preludes?" and I kissed her. Sometimes, after that, I lay with her. We kissed each other's lips and we embraced, but I never entered her. That restraint, which I adhered to religiously—Malkele, I am sure, would have welcomed me, though even she was never bold enough to ask. . . .—that restraint of mine was a crime against my doomed sister. I consider that lack of defiance against the Nazis, and against God too, if you will, my gravest sin. . . .
>
> If we should omit these most private details from the historical record, there is no way to appreciate fully the richness of life for two young Jews, surviving temporarily, with false identifications as Pavel and Maria Witlin, on the Aryan side of Nazi-occupied Warsaw.

For Solomon, the need to go into such explicit detail and thereby create a "historical record" is both personal and professional. He is compelled to establish a record of his sister's life and death in order to come to terms with his own guilt and, as a historian, to replenish the records and lives destroyed by the Nazis and the Diaspora.

- In scenes of illicit sex, at least two things, if not more, must be happening at once: sex and politics, sex and history, sex and defiance.

For Vladimir Nabokov's most infamous creation, Humbert Humbert, nymphetomania is a full-time obsession, though the nitty-gritty of intercourse is something he'd rather not dwell on. Shocking when it was published in the U.S. in 1955, *Lolita* is a complex novel that defies easy characterization: a love story, a satire of American mores and a mock-memoir. Readers were as shocked by Humbert's unabashed hunger for the twelve-year-old daughter of his rooming house landlady, later his wife, as they were by Lolita's casual complicity in these crimes against her.

Nabokov's own obsession here is not sex but language. The density and rhythms of his prose are those of a man panting, a man, as Humbert describes himself while sitting with Lolita, "in a state of excitement bordering on insanity." The prose rocks with suppressed desire; with desire that can't be suppressed; with whimsical, witty, cutting plays on words. But as for the physical details of their copious couplings, Humbert always prefers the clever suggestion to the excessively explicit—and well he should; he is recounting these events from his jail cell. Why draw more attention to the nature of his crimes than he has already had to acknowledge? His account of his first time with Lolita:

> Frigid gentlewomen of the jury! I had thought that months, perhaps years, would elapse before I dared reveal myself to [Lolita]; but by six she was wide awake, and by six fifteen we were technically lovers. I am going to tell you something very strange: it was she who seduced me. . . .
>
> I shall not bore my learned readers with a detailed account of Lolita's presumption. Suffice it to say that not a trace of modesty did I perceive in this beautiful hardly formed young

girl whom modern co-education, juvenile mores, the camp-fire racket and so forth had utterly and hopelessly depraved. She saw the stark act merely as part of a youngster's furtive world, unknown to adults. What adults did for purposes of procreation was no business of hers. My life was handled by little Lo in an energetic, matter-of-fact manner as if it were an insensate gadget unconnected with me. . . . But really these are irrelevant matters; I am not concerned with so-called "sex" at all. Anybody can imagine those elements of animality. A greater endeavor lures me on: to fix once for all the perilous magic of nymphets.

The cost of sexual passion plays a prominent role in the abundant fiction of Joyce Carol Oates. Nowhere is it more prominent or more forbidden than in a novella set at the turn of the century in upstate New York, *I Lock My Door Upon Myself.* It is the story of the forced marriage of an ethereal woman named Calla to a brutal older man. As the result of violent, combative sex, she bears three children and then manages to refuse her husband's entreaties. In a turn of events that shocks her family, her community, and people for miles and generations, she falls in love with Tyrell Thompson, a black man who comes to their house as a water diviner, looking for hidden water deposits with a forked twig. He is the first black she has ever seen and she identifies immediately with the separateness his race imposes on him: *"Like me they are outcasts in this country. No not like me: they are true outcasts."* Her husband tries to kill her, the townsmen bind Tyrell's legs and hurl him in a river (he survives: *"As if it was true, what he'd always boasted—water was his friend and in his power"*), she becomes pregnant with his child, and finally abandons her family. Tyrell asks her to row downstream with him in an old boat he has found "on a day when anyone might see them who chose to see, setting their course deliberately for the falls at Tintern that had not the power—so he boasted, or gave the air of boasting—to withstand Tyrell Thompson's God-given mastery over water."

When they make love moments after he asks her to do this, they are rougher than usual. Calla is startled by the lack of ceremony and afterwards she

> lay dazed, tears running from the corners of her pinched eyes and her entire body aching as if she'd been flung from

a great height to lie here spread-eagled and powerless on her back trusting to a giant of a black man not to smash her bones to bits or smother her with his weight and though now he was saying how he loved her *Oh honey oh honey* she felt her consciousness close to extinction seeing overhead the sky lightly fleeced with clouds, layer upon layer of pale clouds, so empty, so without consolation or even the illusion of such, Calla felt her mouth shaping an involuntary smile.

When had I stopped believing in, what is it—God?—and Jesus Christ His only begotten son? After loving Tyrell Thompson, or before?

This scene, the last of many we see between them, immediately precedes their daredevil boat trip, which results in Tyrell's death and a miscarriage for Calla. The scene is high-pitched, and Tyrell's roughness reflects the violence that has been done to the couple and that they are about to do to themselves. In looking at the sky and realizing she no longer believes in God, Calla is bound even more tightly to Tyrell and their mad trip down the river.

• The scene points again to the need to establish the boundaries and bigotries of the world in which illicit lovers live and thus connect the intensity of the sex scenes between them with their status as outcasts.

LAST WORDS ABOUT THE ILLICIT

Whether your narrator is explicit or elliptical in relating an encounter of forbidden sex, it is up to you to convey the whole complicated picture: who your characters are, where they fit in the culture that forbids sex between them, what kind of culture this is, and what price the characters pay or fear they might for their illicit assignations.

CHAPTER TEN

First Things Last

Solo Sex

"Don't knock it. It's sex with someone you love."　　　　—Woody Allen

"Since Phil Roth has opened up these fields of athletics I suppose it will soon be crowded with young and old men with open flies, beating their wart-colored bones and squirting various quantities of juice onto the wall-paper. But candor is, of course, not all that is needed."

　　　　—John Cheever, *Journals*

A common household item in an English family in the late nineteenth century was a German-made *korsette*, a little metal suit of armor fitted over the genitals, used by nervous Victorian parents to keep children from touching themselves. If, at the close of the twentieth century, twenty-five years after the appearance of Philip Roth's *Portnoy's Complaint*, we like to think of ourselves as less skittish on the subject of masturbation, I am here to remind you that not everyone, myself included, is blasé about the first sexual experience most of us are likely to have and what psychiatrist Thomas Szasz calls "the primary sexual activity of mankind."

Forget literature for the moment and remember the public humiliation of actor Pee-wee Herman, for doing what thousands of unfamous men do every day: masturbate in an X-rated movie theatre. In 1995 the U.S. Surgeon General was fired for remarking that masturbation is a recognized form of human sexuality mentioned in textbooks and should be discussed with high school students. Closer to home, one of the reasons I have saved this chapter for last is because my own uneasiness with the subject made me want to put off writing it as long as I could.

My other reason for leaving it for last is that, though it falls within the definition of sex around which I have organized this book ("Anything that ends in orgasm—if you're lucky, that is"), in its solitary, asocial aspect, it is fundamentally different from the other sexual activities we've looked at up until now.

A compelling sex scene typically involves an *encounter*, characters in the act of moving toward or away from one another, characters *wanting* to be with one another, characters struggling and often failing to make connections. Your characters' desires for one another help plots hurtle forward. Conflict between lovers, or between a pair of lovers and the hostile world, can help make a sex scene sizzle with drama and significance. But when the sexual activity is masturbation, there is no Other to play against, no source of potential conflict from among the dramatis personae.

As sexual activities go, in literature as in life, masturbation has some pretty profound limitations. And though we all may agree, at least sotto voce, that it *is* the primary sexual activity of mankind, there is no getting around the fact that you usually do it when you don't have any better offers. When you are alone (read: lonely, read: abandoned) or when you feel you might as well be. Though it ends in orgasm, if you're lucky, it doesn't do anything to help your social life. Alas, it is often a reminder that you don't have one. (This psychological scenario can be quite different if you are masturbating with a lover, in which case things can be as cozy and cuddly as a Masters and Johnson-approved simultaneous orgasm.)

What does all this have to do with the approaches to writing about sex we have explored up until now? If a good sex scene turns on the relationship between characters, on surprises and dramatic conflict, how can we apply those principles to this activity that, from a dramatic point of view, can be as mechanical and unromantic as urinating?

The answer—the key to all good writing—is to make the writing interesting and make the incident matter. Make it grow out of, connect to, and enlarge your characters and your story. Why write about it if it doesn't?

Look at the general principles in chapters two and three and see how many of them you can apply to writing fiction about masturbating.

(All of them, I think.) Then add these four new principles and study the examples that follow, including scenes by two student writers who came to my attention while researching this book.

1. Yes, you do it to yourself, but that doesn't mean you have to be alone. Quite often in fiction—and masturbation too—the more the merrier. When an author moves this most solitary of activities into a group setting, possibilities for drama, conflict, character development and plot follow right along. Sure, a character alone can have an interesting interior life, but two characters together can make sparks fly, whether they're making love, masturbating or solving a murder. Remember the scene in Federico Fellini's autobiographical film, *Amarcord*, in which a group of horny, rowdy teenage boys sets a car rocking and makes its headlights blink in something like orgasmic excitement with their boisterous collective handiwork? In Alice Lukens' example on page 136, a group of fifth-grade girls who masturbate on gym ropes and, as a result, call themselves the Vine Sisters, add a new twist to female bonding. And in the example below from Dorothy Allison's novel, *Bastard Out of Carolina*, Ruth Anne's tacit understanding with her sister about their common activity, which they sometimes practice while sleeping in the same bed, allows them a glancing closeness that nothing else in their relationship permits.

2. Don't ignore your uneasy feelings. If you have uneasy feelings about masturbation, you don't have to bury them to write about it. As Dorothy Allison has told us, "Write to your fear." Explore your uncomfortable feelings, use them, exploit them. Bequeath them to your characters. Make a character's shyness, guilt, or fear of getting caught part of the drama.

3. Just write it. You'll have plenty of time to rewrite later—or to learn to live with your embarrassment. In my interview with novelist Joseph Olshan, he spoke a great deal about how "scary" it was for him to write explicitly gay sex scenes in his fifth and latest novel, *Nightswimmer*. Though we were speaking generally about the sex scenes in *Nightswimmer*, because it includes a bold and moving masturbation scene, I want to include some of his comments in this context:

> I wrote some scenes and I thought, "Oh, my God, I can't believe I wrote this." But I just forced myself to do it. And even now parts of it just make me cringe. . . . I remember a

description of when this character finally has anal sex and I thought, "What is my father going to say when he reads this?" At the end of the semester, one of my students said she had read my novel early in the semester and I thought, "Oh, my God, she read that scene!" When you're sitting down to write, you have to banish all those thoughts and think: This may go but I need to just do it and get it out. It may be that I don't think it's appropriate ultimately but it's an exercise now. I can see how far I can go, and that's how I do it. But if I really believed it might be published, I think I would find myself having a hard time with it.

An excerpt and discussion of the masturbation scene from *Nightswimmer* appear later in this chapter.

4. The absence of a partner means fantasy plays a greater role than it does in sex for two or more. Without a sex partner, we have to invent our own. Without another person to hold onto, our thoughts while masturbating are certain to fix on something besides world peace and baseball scores. In a passage typical of the over-the-top tone of *Portnoy's Complaint*, Alex Portnoy admits to one of his masturbation fantasies, helped along with an improvised sex aid:

> On an outing of our family association, I once cored an apple, saw to my astonishment (and with the aid of my obsession) what it looked like, and ran off into the woods to fall upon the orifice of the fruit, pretending that the cool and mealy hole was actually between the legs of that mythical being who always called me Big Boy when she pleaded for what no girl in all recorded history had ever had. "Oh shove it in me, Big Boy," cried the cored apple that I banged silly on that picnic.

GIVEN CIRCUMSTANCES

1. Everyone does it. No one wants to talk about it.
2. People are often made uncomfortable reading about it.
3. If you are alone, you don't want to get caught or leave evidence. If you are with others, you generally don't want to be found out by those outside the group.

4. Fantasy typically plays a larger role in masturbation than in "group sex."
5. It has historically been more openly accepted, expected, discussed and joked about by males than by females.
6. Masturbation can be a powerful source of solace.
7. It can also be an irrefutable, even if transient, reminder of loneliness, and the shame of loneliness.

EXAMPLES

A character's feelings about his or her masturbation are often an important element of the scene in which it is depicted, whether an author conveys them directly or indirectly. Ruth Anne Boatwright, narrator of *Bastard Out of Carolina,* Dorothy Allison's powerful novel of incest and family violence, is as blunt in expressing her feelings on masturbation as she is in everything else. As a girl Ruth Anne is raped and repeatedly beaten by her stepfather, Daddy Glen, as her mother listens on the other side of a door, washes the girl's face afterwards, and urges her "not to be so stubborn, not to make him mad." When Ruth Anne begins to masturbate, in the bedroom she shares with her sister, she fantasizes people watching Daddy Glen beat her, creating a tortured connection between the violence done to her and the pleasure she wants to give herself. She narrates using language that combines the child's terror and longing with the adult's more cool-eyed understanding of the complex dynamics far beyond a child's comprehension:

> When he beat me, I screamed and kicked and cried like the baby I was: But sometimes when I was safe and alone, I would imagine the ones who watched. Someone had to watch—some girl I admired who barely knew I existed, some girl from church or down the street. . . . In my imagination I was proud and defiant. I'd stare back at him with my teeth set, making no sound at all, no shameful scream, no begging. Those who watched admired me and hated him. I pictured it that way and put my hands between my legs. It was scary, but it was thrilling too. Those who watched me, loved me. It was as if I was being beaten for them. I was wonderful in their eyes. . . .
>
> I was ashamed of myself for the things I thought about

when I put my hands between my legs, more ashamed for masturbating to the fantasy of being beaten than for being beaten in the first place. I lived in a world of shame. I hid my bruises as if they were evidence of crimes I had committed. I knew I was a sick disgusting person. I couldn't stop my step-father from beating me, but *I* was the one who masturbated. *I* did that, and how could I explain to anyone that I hated being beaten but still masturbated to the story I told myself about it?

Yet . . . I loved those fantasies, even though I was sure they were a terrible thing. They had to be; they were self-centered and they made me have shuddering orgasms. In them, I was very special. I was triumphant, important. I was not ashamed. There was no heroism possible in the real beatings. There was just being beaten until I was covered with snot and misery.

Later in the novel, Ruth Anne discovers her sister is also mastur-bating often, sometimes while they are in the bed they share at night. When they return from school in the afternoons, they have a tacit agreement to give each other time alone in the bedroom. One after-noon, Ruth Anne walks in on her sister and finds her with a pair of their mother's underpants covering her face. In their conspiracy of silence and shame, Ruth Anne grabs a book she had been reading and pretends not to have seen anything. During this period the sisters barely speak to one another, "but we made sure no one else ever went in the bedroom when one of us was there alone."

Allison's emphasis throughout is *not* on the details of stimulation; the narrative does not lead toward the orgasm. How could it? The pleasurable physical sensations are so tainted and twisted by Ruth Anne's memories and disturbing fantasies that masturbating is a kind of self-inflicted punishment that she nevertheless cannot stop doing. The narrative moves instead toward insight and illumination, to an understanding of what these events and moments felt like to Ruth Anne as a child and how she makes sense of them now looking back.

Ruth Anne is as candid when writing about masturbation as she is when relating her stepfather's brutality or her mother's divided loyalties; she makes no attempts to prettify, to gloss over humiliations, to make her characters look better than they are.

In the scene with the sister, Allison explores one of the given circumstances of masturbation: that we don't want to be found out. The sisters are found out by each other, but the furtive nature of the act means there will not be a confrontation. The passages are especially moving because they hint at a loyalty and intimacy between the girls that is not expressed or acknowledged otherwise. Their unspoken secret seems to be the only basis for any closeness between them.

- These scenes remind us that masturbation scenes, like all good sex scenes, cannot be plunked down in the middle of a story either to titillate or take up space. They must be stitched in, so they connect to the larger concerns of the work.

If masturbation is fraught with anguish and guilt for Ruth Anne Boatwright, in the very different universe of Alice Lukens, it is a source of female bonding, group giggles, and only fleeting embarrassment. These passages are from *The Vine Sisters*, a collection of short stories Lukens wrote for her senior thesis in creative writing at Princeton University. These are the only scenes I have come across in which female characters acknowledge and celebrate group masturbation.

In this scene from a story in the collection also called "The Vine Sisters," narrator Kate describes what happens after lunch at her girls' private school:

Sometimes, to goof off, we swung from vine to vine like Tarzan and Jane. We hung upside down from the branches and did flips, our uniform skirts falling down around our faces. Our shirts came untucked and our socks fell down around our ankles and nobody was there to yell at us or give us detentions for it. But mostly, we went to get It.

I first discovered It in first grade one day, climbing a pole. I got It climbing trees and ropes and rocks, rubbing against an old wooden horse in the playground, shimmying up swingset poles, rubbing against doors at home, my bedpost, my bureau, my pillows, my stuffed animals. Kay could get It by just crossing and uncrossing her legs. I couldn't get It that way, or only a little bit, not like on a rope. Kay said she saw her older sister crossing and uncrossing her legs sometimes in the kitchen when she didn't know Kay was looking. Diana,

Beth, and I didn't have sisters, just brothers. But both Diana and Beth, like me, said they had known about It a long time, for as long as they could remember.

We discovered each other in gym classes in fourth grade, climbing ropes. I wouldn't let myself feel It until the very top, not until I touched the ceiling. Then I would let myself sit there for a little while, just hanging and feeling It between my legs and looking down on everyone on the gym floor. I noticed when Diana and Kay climbed they would do the same thing, shimmy way up the rope and then just hang there, moving their legs a little bit, looking down at everybody. That's how I knew. We were the only three who could climb all the way up the rope and touch the ceiling. . . .

We called ourselves the Vine Sisters. We had two member-ship requirements: It, and secrecy. Sometimes in the middle of class somebody would say "it," talking about something entirely different, and we would look at each other and laugh and think *if only they knew*. Sometimes even thinking about it was enough to make It do a somersault or two between our legs.

A year later, in fifth grade, Kate notices a new shy girl on the ropes who also seems to have It, and she and a few other Vine Sisters try to "recruit a new member, Cary." They led her to the bathroom for a grilling:

> "We want to ask you a question," said Kay.
> "Okay," Cary said.
> "When you climb ropes," I blurted, "do you feel some-thing between your legs?"
> "We all do," said Beth, "so don't worry if you do."
> Cary surprised us all and started to cry.
> "Don't cry!" Kay cried out. "We all feel it! It's wonderful! We have a club. We call ourselves the Vine Sisters and—"
> The door to the bathroom swung open, and Ms. Richter, our math teacher, entered. We hushed up and grinned.

Cary runs from them and the Vine Sisters confer, wishing "she weren't so ashamed," but deciding that she probably won't get them into trouble because "she's so embarrassed she can't even talk to us." They decide to quit their recruiting efforts and maintain the secret society.

Though the Vine Sisters are not embarrassed by what they do in each other's presence, they know that It is taboo, and It must be kept a secret. The author uses the secret status of the group to create enough dramatic tension to move the story forward and sow conflict between characters (the group and Cary, the group and Ms. Richter).

The most engaging surprise to me in these passages is the narrator's breezy openness on the subject. She is atypically plucky, unabashed, and seemingly without shame or embarrassment in her pursuits of It. And the fact that It is not just her own private pleasure but a conspiracy of pleasure, a private club that, CIA-like, operates furtively in public, creates ripples of literary pleasure for the reader.

This example is from a short story, "Spot-the-Ball," by Ian McGuire, a British graduate student at the University of Virginia. The story is narrated by a man who recounts scenes from his childhood and reimagines and invents scenes from his father's youth, including his time in 1944, at age eighteen, in Cairo, serving in the Royal Corps of Signalmen. By imagining moments that his father surely did not relate to him in such detail, the son hopes to penetrate his father's early unhappiness and the adult life of quiet desperation in which the son was raised. At one point, the narrator imagines his father at thirteen with his own father, his father thinking that "the two of them are only different versions of each other." The narrator must surely fear his own identification with his despairing father, and in attempting to understand his father's unhappiness, he is also searching for the origins of his own.

In this scene from Cairo during World War II, the narrator describes his father and his father's twenty-two-year-old fellow radio-operator, Jenkins, whom the narrator describes (on whose authority, one wonders) as "rosy-cheeked and well-hung." "Occasionally when they are sitting at their radios, each facing the opposite wall, drenched with sweat, burdened with flies and the acrid smell of overheated bakelite, Jenkins will lean back, rub his crotch and exclaim that he feels like a wank. My father will push him away, tell him to bugger off."

But at night (the narrator/son imagines):

They lie on camp beds six feet apart. The tops of their cigarettes glow and fade <u>like a slow version of the morse code they collect all day</u>. Outside the hut there is at first nothing, then, a long way off, the war. The moon is <u>horned and yellow as a toe-nail</u>. In these minutes or hours before sleep my father feels porous and prone to collapse, ready to crumble under the wash of time which moves through him without hesitation, recognition, concern.

Jenkins unzips and starts to wank. The movement of his hand is lugubrious and fluid. At the same time he blows smoke out of the corner of his mouth, half-heartedly sucks his teeth, and looks, incuriously, about the room. He has <u>the air of someone who is waiting for a bus—as if, at any moment, he might begin to whistle</u>.

Without turning his head my father watches. Flies dot his mosquito net <u>like raisins on pudding</u>, and it is so hot that <u>the air feels stewed</u>. They have been there three weeks and this is a more or less nightly routine—Jenkins's gelatinous body petting itself, urging itself on—which hardly touches him any more. Jenkins encourages my father to join in if he likes, but he never does, preferring himself the noisome darkness of the latrines, the emptiness of the desert.

All of a sudden Jenkins's body jolts slightly <u>as if a clutch has been engaged</u>. He arches his neck, rolls back his eyes; his mouth is a little "o". It is <u>as if he is working on the part of an engine he cannot see</u>, and he has to proceed solely by his sense of touch. His movements become first fidgety, then frenetic, finally there is a splat of sperm on his hairless chest and an exclamation: "By gum I'm full of it tonight!", in the broad cartoonish Lancashire of a music-hall comic.

It seems to my father, in his state of contrived distraction, <u>his own penis as narrow and woody as a snooker cue</u>, that Egypt, Africa, is entirely dissolved by Jenkins's bluffness, and that it only re-forms gradually around them after he has nodded noisily off, his still-slick hand lolling decadently out of the net, being punctured, punctured, punctured, by mosquitoes. [My underscoring]

The great strengths of this scene are its highly specific, detailed images and descriptions, with an emphasis on unusual metaphors, which I have underlined. The result is that every gesture McGuire describes is exceptionally vivid and original, allowing us to consider the familiar motions of masturbating from a very unfamiliar perspective. Yet because we know this is the narrator's fantasy, not an account of "what really happened," the level of detail and invention has a haunting, almost surreal quality.

The strangeness of this scene, both the descriptions and the fact that it's a son's invented memories, should not keep us from seeing the instructional value of it. It reminds us to create images and metaphors that convey both the mechanics and the mood of every sexual encounter. In this case, the images are so arresting that we must read the passage slowly and pause to visualize each new gesture, which thrusts us into the strangeness and isolation of this universe at every turn.

Though the (usually) solitary nature of masturbation prevents much conflict from developing between characters, in this scene McGuire creates subtle tensions by exploring the differences in temperament between Jenkins and the narrator's father. Though what *happens* in this scene is that one fellow wanks while the other watches, the scene is *about* the differences between Jenkins and the narrator's passive, despairing father, between Jenkins' "bluffness," which is powerful enough to dissolve Africa, and the father's failure to rise to Jenkins' offer, his failure to achieve what the narrator later calls "Jenkins' condition of cock-sure cheeriness, of goatish inner peace." Jenkins' masturbation and his invitation to join in are a metaphor for openness to sensation and adventure, which the narrator's father declines then and always, settling instead for the gloom and despair in which the narrator grew up.

Ian McGuire plays cleverly with the idea of masturbation fantasies. Typically, it is the person masturbating who fantasizes in order to become aroused. In this case, the narrator fantasizes someone else's masturbation not in order to be aroused but in order to come to some understanding of his own history.

This excerpt from Joseph Olshan's mournful novel about gay New York in the 1990s combines telephone sex and Call Waiting, which many people, including narrator Will Kaplan, find almost equally thrilling. Late one night, Will has called a telephone sex line where he speaks at length to his "phone sex partner," and begins to masturbate, coming close to orgasm, when he is interrupted by Call Waiting. He takes the call, hoping it is his new lover, and finds instead the jealous friend, Peter, who introduced Will to the new lover. After exchanging some sharp words, Will clicks off, intending to call back the phone sex line. But there is no need to; Will finds the man still on the line, courtesy of Call Waiting:

> I'd already forgotten his name. Not that it mattered, because he'd probably given me a phony name anyway.
>
> "Wow!" I said, "you waited." I felt an amazing tenderness for this disembodied voice who probably lied about the way he looked, but who was obviously patient, maybe even steadfast. Suddenly I thought I could feel his loneliness there in the outlying borough that bordered La Guardia Airport and Flushing Bay, a residential area dismissed by the Manhattan elite as being déclassé. And it occurred to me, as I began urging myself and this guy toward a late-night climax, that perhaps I could persuade him to become my monogamous phone lover.

What *happens* in this scene is that Will masturbates on the telephone with a stranger, but what the scene is *about* is the power of loneliness to draw people together.

Here again, Olshan's emphasis is not on the progress of the orgasm but on the mood, the emotional and cultural ambience, the far-reaching loneliness of the big city, the disembodied voices, the tiny lies we tell each other in order to connect across these chasms. The paragraph ends with a wonderful, haunting irony: that you could be faithful to the disembodied voice of a stranger on your telephone. Instead of a masturbation fantasy that summons a person, this dreamer yearns only for a loyal voice on the phone—perhaps the ideal sex partner in the age of AIDS.

LAST WORDS ABOUT FIRST THINGS

Make sure your masturbation scenes are about something besides the mechanics of wanking. Because masturbation creates such an array of unsettling feelings in most people—your characters and readers alike—give us a clue or two, even if they are indirect, about how your characters feel about what they are doing. To tackle your own uneasy feelings, take Dorothy Allison's advice and write to your fear: Explore and exploit these uneasy feelings. Bequeath them to your characters.

The close of a chapter on solitary sex seems an appropriate place to wrap things up. Now that we have mentioned the final unmentionable, it is time to overcome your lingering uncertainty, the last vestiges of your skittishness over writing about sex, and show your demons the door without further adieu. It is time to roll up your sleeves, fix a fresh pot of coffee, slip a fresh diskette into the computer, and plan to be late for dinner.

EXERCISES

1. "I could never tell anyone _____ ." (Fill in the blank and write until you feel you have explored this secret in detail.) This is an exercise Dorothy Allison routinely gives her students. The blank does not have to have anything to do with sex. It also does not need to be true.

2. Given circumstances. Chapters five through ten focus on specific sexual relationships—between first-time lovers, married people, adulterers, etc.—and what they mean for the fiction writer. Here are five other possible sexual relationships. For each one, write a list of given circumstances (characteristics that are true in every or almost every case) and comb your memory for examples from novels or short stories. Consult the examples you remembered and see how many of your given circumstances apply:

   a. Sex partners for the purposes of conception;
   b. Sex partners for hire;
   c. Sex between partners of very different ages;
   d. Sex between people who were lovers when they were much younger, have been separated, and are meeting again in old age;
   e. Sex between people who were once married but are no longer.

3. Write your own. The best sex scenes arise from the needs, histories and compulsions of your characters. But for practice purposes, write a few free-standing sex scenes and see what you come up with. Begin with the types of sexual relationships listed above. For each type of relationship, write two scenes, one intended to be funny and one not funny. Include well-defined, clearly motivated characters, plenty of details, at least a little conflict, a few surprises and dialogue where necessary.

4. Explicit vs. discreet. Experiment with the sex scenes you have written above. First, make them more sexually explicit than they are now, then less explicit. Look at all the versions a week later and see what works and what doesn't work. Look again a month later. Have your perceptions and judgments changed?

5. Talk to me. Write a sex scene using only dialogue. We should come to the end of the scene knowing who the characters are, what they want or wanted from the encounter, what they want in a broader sense, and whether they have gotten what they wanted. The dialogue should also reveal where the scene is taking place: what part of the world, what room, etc.

6. Location, location, location. Write a sex scene in which the sense of place is central to the encounter. Sense of place = geography and actual spot: the room, the bench, the bridge underpass.

7. Sex and death. Proximity to death profoundly alters our experience of life. Write a sex scene between people who are or have recently been affected by death or the threat of death. It could be war, an illness, accident or a natural disaster.

8. Monologues. Write a monologue in which the speaker recounts a sexual experience that ended differently from how he or she thought it would end. As always, we should know who the characters are, what they want, and what the setting has to do with the sex.

Elizabeth Benedict, a graduate of Barnard College, is the author of the novels *Safe Conduct* (Farrar, Straus & Giroux, 1993); *The Beginner's Book of Dreams* (Alfred A. Knopf, 1988); and *Slow Dancing* (Alfred A. Knopf, 1985), which was a finalist for the American Book Award. Her short story "Feasting," published in *The Massachusetts Review,* was chosen for *Prize Stories: The O. Henry Awards.* She has written book reviews, essays and travel features for *The New York Times, Boston Globe, Washington Post, Los Angeles Times, Esquire* and other publications; and personal commentaries for National Public Radio's *All Things Considered.* She has taught at Swarthmore and Haverford Colleges, the University of Iowa Writers' Workshop, and is currently on the faculty of Princeton University's Creative Writing Program.

INDEX